Discovering the Culture of Childhood

Discovering *the* Culture *of* Childhood

Emily Plank

Redleaf Press®
www.redleafpress.org
800-423-8309

Published by Redleaf Press
10 Yorkton Court
St. Paul, MN 55117
www.redleafpress.org

First edition 2016
Cover design by Erin Kirk New
Cover photograph by Getty Images/iStock/Nastia11
Interior design by Douglas Schmitz
Typeset in Garamond
Printed in the United States of America
23 22 21 20 19 18 17 16   1 2 3 4 5 6 7 8

Library of Congress Cataloging-in-Publication Data
Names: Plank, Emily, author.
Title: Discovering the culture of childhood / Emily Plank.
Description: St. Paul, MN : Redleaf Press, 2016. | Includes bibliographical
   references and index.
Identifiers: LCCN 2016003407 (print) | LCCN 2016014845 (ebook) | ISBN
   9781605544625 (paperback) | ISBN 9781605544632 ()
Subjects: LCSH: Children—Social conditions. | Children—Cross-cultural
   studies. | BISAC: SOCIAL SCIENCE / Children's Studies. | FAMILY &
   RELATIONSHIPS / Life Stages / Infants & Toddlers. | EDUCATION /
   Professional Development. | PSYCHOLOGY / Developmental / Child.
Classification: LCC HQ767.9 .P625 2016 (print) | LCC HQ767.9 (ebook) |
   DDC
   305.23—dc23
LC record available at http://lccn.loc.gov/2016003407

Printed on acid-free paper

⁓ೞ ೞ⁓

*For Ezra, who believes in me relentlessly.
And for Tekoa, Simone, and Desmond,
who have inspired this book.*

⁓ೞ ೞ⁓

Contents

Foreword

"CHILDREN ARE NOT IMPERFECT HUMANS, but they are imperfect adults." This is my favorite quote from *Discovering the Culture of Childhood,* one I jotted down as I read. In this vibrant and dynamic first book, Emily Plank treats us to many such provocative statements about young children and our understanding (or misunderstanding) of their behaviors, motives, and capabilities. Plank suggests that many of us measure children according to the level of adultness they have attained, placing them on a continuum of development that focuses on what they will become rather than what they are capable of today.

In doing so, she cautions us, we can fail to see what children truly need and reach the wrong conclusions about both their motives and their behaviors. All of us have seen this failure in our work with children, among our own families, or anyplace where small children and adults gather. Parents and other caregivers want their children to behave, but they often don't understand that there simply is no misbehavior in the earliest years. It is all just behavior. Reminding ourselves that children think and act differently than we do can empower us to respond in more thoughtful and supportive ways to these inevitable happenings. As Plank comments, "Viewing childhood as a distinct culture shifts the nature of adult/child relationships from one of hierarchy and power to one of mutual respect."

This book serves as a call to action for all adults to consider changing their thinking about childhood. Why should we tell children to say "I'm sorry" if they are not? Why does one have to color only with the point of a crayon? Most of us have feigned illness once or twice when we were just too tired to join a friend for dinner, yet we are horrified when a four-year-old growls at another at preschooler, "*Go away*—I want to be by myself!" Emily Plank encourages us to believe that in truly understanding young children, we will resist the urge to interrupt, punish, script, overrule, manipulate, and dictate their play (and behavior).

This fascinating volume covers many topics, such as language and artistic expression, children's friendships, and approaches to child discipline and guidance. Plank also explains the price children are paying in loss of play and environments for play due to a national trend of focusing more attention on academics than on social and emotional development. Of course, not every reader will agree with every suggestion. Programs in the United States are so varied that those in large centers where lunch is served on the work tables and sleep mats are laid out in the block area will find it harder to imagine postponing cleanup time to leave "works in progress" than family programs, which are often not as bound by some of the restrictions to which larger programs must adhere. Our own temperaments and experiences affect how comfortable we are with art experiences that are void of adult direction.

As a college ECE instructor for more than thirty years, I'd like to see *Discovering the Culture of Childhood* on the required reading list right up there with *Introduction to Child Growth and Development*. It is a must read for all who teach children, have children, or work with children—especially for those who write about or teach all of the above.

Carol Garhart Mooney

SparkNH & Project LAUNCH
Author of *Theories of Childhood: An Introduction to Dewey, Montessori, Erikson, Piaget & Vygotsky*

Acknowledgments

I WOULD LIKE TO EXPRESS my heartfelt gratitude to all those who have helped make this book a reality. Thank you to everyone at Redleaf Press who believed in this project and helped bring it to print, including Laurie Herrmann, Kyra Ostendorf, and my wonderful editor, Danny Miller. I am honored to be a Redleaf author.

Thank you to Tom, Melissa, Lakisha, Marc, Kelly, and Denita, who contributed such wonderful and rich stories for this book.

To those who gave me opportunities to grow as a leader in the field of early childhood education: the Iowa Association for the Education of Young Children, in particular Barb and those involved with the Emerging Leader program; Child Care Resource and Referral of Southeast Iowa, especially Kristin and Tessa; and Community Coordinated Child Care in Iowa City, in particular Susan and Mary. Thank you all for affirming my voice and contribution to the field.

To friends and colleagues who offered time discussing my early ideas or reading initial drafts, sharing both feedback and encouragement, and to those who gave me a road map to move this book from my head to a publisher to print, especially Ijumaa, Kelly, Heather, and Peg.

Thank you in particular to my dear friend Kelly Matthews. Your real-time text updates while you read and edited my initial manuscript, our coordinated phone conversations across many time zones, and your endless encouragement and validation confirmed that this project was important for our field. Your belief in me and in my work has truly been a source of strength through this process.

To all the wonderful families and children with whom I have worked over the years at Abundant Life Family Child Care, thank you for letting me be a part of your lives, and thank you for teaching me about the culture of childhood.

I owe the most gratitude to my family. To Ezra, for helping me refine my ideas, editing various drafts, shouldering extra responsibilities with our family so I could write, and, most important, believing that I could do this. And to my amazing children, who shared their joy and love with me as I went along. I love you.

"Becoming Outsiders"
An Invitation

"The only true voyage of discovery, the only fountain of eternal youth, would not be to visit strange lands, but to possess other eyes, to behold the universe through the eyes of another, of a hundred others, to behold the hundred universes that each of them beholds, that each of them is."

—Marcel Proust

MY FIRST PASSPORT ARRIVED IN THE MAIL when I was nineteen and preparing to study abroad in Germany for the year. My uncertainty about this new adventure grew as my departure date approached. I remember boarding the bus at the Frankfurt airport following my long international flight and riding the final stretch of the journey to my new home away from home in Heidelberg. The sky was overcast and gray; lush green hillsides were dotted with iconic German architecture and the ruins of ancient castles. My heart raced as I rode along the autobahn.

As a traveling novice, I erroneously assumed that Germany would be a lot like the United States, but with a different language, cuisine, and currency.

I was so wrong.

Surprisingly, what I noticed first were the clotheslines hanging outside nearly every home and apartment. It was as if the hanging laundry opened up a new world I had never considered: if German citizens with the financial means to *own* a dryer elected *not* to dry their clothing in a machine, what else was different in this new country?

There were small differences such as the fact that Germans ate pizza and sandwiches with a fork and knife, purchased milk in cardboard boxes arranged on store shelves rather than in coolers, and did not add a tip to the bill in restaurants. There were also larger differences; for example, strangers did not smile at each other when they passed on the streets, and there was a marked absence of small talk in all situations where I expected it. Each time I encountered a difference, it made me aware of my own ways of acting. Before living in Germany, I never realized how much the Americans in my community smiled at or chitchatted with strangers—passersby on the streets, the people sharing a line in the grocery store, or seat neighbors on public transportation. There was some kind of unwritten code that we all knew by heart: while checking out at the grocery store, engage in small talk with the cashier; when sitting on the bus, greet the people around you; smile sweetly at passengers with small children. I realize now—though I didn't at the time—that my unwritten code of behavior is not shared equally by everyone in the world, and not even by everyone in my immediate home community, but it was only when I lived in a culture that did not share my behaviors that I could reflect on my unconscious beliefs.

The cultural differences I observed while living in Germany awakened me to an idea I had never entertained before: I had membership in a culture with a set of beliefs unique to my context. It was as if I looked in the mirror for the first time! Before I traveled, my unchallenged perspectives were the standard by which all other behavior was measured. I thought everyone would respond the way I did in certain situations. As Barbara Rogoff says in her book *The Cultural Nature of Human Development*, "Cultural processes surround all of us and often involve subtle, tacit, taken-for-granted events and ways of doing things that require open eyes, ears, and minds to notice and understand" (2003, 11).

I have experienced Rogoff's words to be true. When I remain in a fairly constant community, my ways of doing things go unquestioned. For example, I was at a restaurant once with a friend and we shared a meal. We split the bill at the end and I made a calculation error, inadvertently leaving a small tip. The service had been satisfactory; I had no reason to intentionally short-change the server. Still, she followed us out the door that evening asking, "Was something wrong with the service?" My behavior—leaving a small tip—was interpreted as dissatisfaction. From within a culture where tipping is customary, that interpretation was a logical one.

The tricky part about culture is that it most often exists below surface-level interactions. Tatsushi Arai, in an essay on cultural fluency, explains culture like this: "Cultural assumptions internalized in our unconscious are like unknowingly wearing a pair of yellow glasses, turning everything blue into green, and red into orange. We disagree with cultural others wearing eyeglasses of different colors, without ever understanding the different glasses. Instead we wonder why these cultural outsiders can never accept even the simplest fact that green is green and orange is orange!" (2006, 59) This is exactly what I learned on that first trip to Germany: my lenses had a unique color and shaped my view of the world.

Some of our cultural understandings are explicitly taught. When I was growing up, my parents explained the process of tipping at restaurants, and they showed me how to use the total bill to calculate an appropriate tip for adequate service. But most of what we think of as normal behavior becomes that in our minds imperceptibly, over time, and beneath the surface. I know the rules of my culture because I am an insider. Through observations I made growing up in my specific context, I formed my behavior. I observe my friends eating pizza without a fork and knife, and I know to eat pizza gracefully with my hands. I observe pedestrians yielding the right-of-way to vehicle traffic; I yield the right-of-way to vehicle traffic.

When I found myself in Germany in the fall of my sophomore year of college and began to notice the subtle and not-so-subtle differences between the Germans and myself, I started to understand that behavior exists within a cultural context. The Germans I encountered in public behaved in ways that were unexpected to me as an American, and in order to draw the right conclusions about what their behaviors meant, I would need to recognize that my lens for assessing behavior was framed by my cultural experiences. Just as I might mistakenly think my German neighbors were unfriendly for not smiling, I was surprised to find that the Germans I met often misinterpreted the "overly smiley" Americans as shallow because they smiled at anyone—even people they didn't know—on the streets! To say that Germans were unfriendly because we didn't exchange a passing smile was just as inaccurate as saying I was shallow for smiling. All human beings possess a lens through which they interpret the actions of other human beings; it is being aware of one's own lens that is the hard part.

Despite my pre-Germany jitters, the year I spent living outside the United States was one of the most transformational experiences of my young adult life. It wasn't always effortless, but I returned home to the United States with a new confidence and an understanding of my place in the global community. While living in Germany, I lacked an accurate interpretive lens. My community was relatively static in my growing-up years: I lived in the same house until I went to college, attended the same school with the same friends, and did the same things for fun on the weekends. I assumed my beliefs and behaviors were somewhat universal because everyone I knew behaved by a more-or-less similar set of rules. My cultural beliefs were the yardstick by which all other behaviors were measured. All of that changed when I began to travel and encounter people with different cultural frameworks from my own. I started to recognize that I was wearing a distinct set of cultural "glasses," and I started to see the complex diversity of cultures that existed within my home community.

I no longer believed that I existed *outside* a culture, but I recognized my membership *within* one.

More than a decade after I first set foot outside my home country, I was traveling with my young family in Japan. Now an experienced traveler, I was eager to expose my children to the euphoria that comes with immersion in a different culture. I find bustling streets of unfamiliar sounds, restaurant menus in new languages, and grocery stores filled with unfamiliar food electrifying.

What I was not prepared for were the escalators in the Japanese underground metro system. Imagine thousands of people, walking at a near run, hustling to and from train platforms to move about the city. Families, professional commuters, and Buddhist monks all knew the expectation: when riding the escalators, form a perfect single-file line on the left, leaving an open lane on the right for people who were running to catch a train. The actual process of riding the escalator was nothing extraordinary, but observing the ritual by which people moved from one place to the next, I was struck by the realization that I had changed. Without verbal or written instructions, I could appropriately engage in the Japanese escalator culture: even though such formality regarding escalator behavior was not a custom in my culture in the United States, I knew to stand on the left because I watched the Japanese stand on the left. But my experience was more than that. I knew to stand on the left because I knew to pay attention to the behavior of the insiders.

In my early years as a traveler in Germany, I didn't know to pay attention. I didn't see myself as an outsider because that would have required me to understand I was an insider in my own culture. Instead, I was an unreflective, unaware tourist. Tourists hover over a culture, visiting significant places and taking selfies in the expected locations for their Facebook newsfeeds. Tourists have bucket lists of sights they are trying to cross off and travel guides to help them find the hidden treasures in new places. Tourists stay at arm's length from the culture and do not actively seek to understand. Self-aware outsiders engage, even at the superficial level of noting escalator behavior and adapting to the cultural expectations. As an outsider, I can still see the sights or consult travel guides for information, and I have plenty of selfies to prove I was in Japan. But the manner in which I engaged with the culture was fundamentally different than my behavior would have been a decade earlier. As a tourist, I would have boarded the escalators and stood where I wanted—not out of malice or a desire to mess up the order of things, but because I didn't know what I didn't know. I would have likely missed that there was a cultural expectation at all in this interaction.

Outsiders know that they don't know anything, but they know to ask, or to simply wonder within themselves about the behaviors they see. Outsiders are familiar with the feelings of being out of place. Outsiders look to insiders for help, relying on observation for clues about appropriate behavior. Outsiders walk lightly and refrain from making judgments about what they experience, knowing that without context, their conclusions are likely inaccurate. Outsiders give insiders the benefit of the doubt, attributing the best possible motivation to behavior that may seem off-putting or rude. To an outsider, the unfamiliar leads to what Venashri Pillay calls *surprise*: "Surprise happens when our expectations are not met. Rather than dismissing or explaining surprises away, it is good to follow them, seeing them as tributaries of the river. It is likely that divergent values or meanings are animating the behavior that surprises us. With a spirit of inquiry, we seek to learn more rather than using our frames of reference to judge the differences that led to our surprise" (Pillay 2006, 289). As I have become a more frequent traveler, I encounter this type of surprise more and more often.

It was there—on the subway platform in Japan—that I realized I had made the shift. I was no longer strictly a tourist; I had become a self-aware outsider. I stood for a moment, having a sort of out-of-body experience, and absorbing the gravity of my enlightenment.

And that's when it happened. The idea for this book engulfed me like a wave. I clearly saw a parallel between my place as an outsider in the metro stop and my role as an outsider with children. The lens through which I see the world is not just *American* or *female* or *middle-class* or *Californian*; the lens is also *adult*. The lenses that my children have are entirely different because they are members of a separate culture. My children and I share a common culture of race, ethnicity, ability, geography, and socioeconomic class, but we are situated in entirely different cultures demarcated by age. The same dispositions I need to engage respectfully with the Japanese culture, I need to engage respectfully with young children. My failed attempts at fitting in when I travel are connected to my failed attempts at working successfully with young children. It would be awhile before the wave of understanding I experienced in Japan grew into this book, but I can trace its roots back to my escalator moment.

Since my year of living in Germany, I have logged many miles traveling the world. Living in France, Switzerland, and on a ship sailing the world; traveling to faraway places like Thailand and Morocco; and developing an awareness of the rich diversity of cultures that exist within the United States, I have built an understanding of what it can look like to relate cross-culturally with others who are different from me. I have gained powerful skills of observation when entering a new culture. I have learned to pay attention to the different social cues as a way to bring my behavior into line with what is expected. I have learned to invite the "surprise" when something strikes me as odd. I have developed the confidence to engage thoughtfully with insiders as a way to learn about how their assumptions are formed.

A New Lens for Childhood

My new challenge, and the focus of this book, is to illuminate the unnamed cross-cultural relationship that exists between adults and children. In my work as an early childhood educator, I notice striking similarities between my experiences with young children and my time spent traveling. We—the adults who are charged with caring for young children—often lack the resources to truly understand the behavior of young children. Just as I assumed Germans were somehow Americans with a different language, so do adults often tacitly assume children are mini-versions of themselves. We hold children to adult standards of acting—such as being quiet, still, or tidy, or watching where they are going—without stopping to examine the reasons why adult standards are the yardstick that defines all human behavior. We use adult language to describe the personalities of young children, such as claiming they are "flirtatious," "bossy," "mean," "naughty," or "bullies." Our adult intention is not to malign young children or their behavior; we simply lack the ability to view and appreciate childhood as a separate culture. But regardless of how noble our intentions are, the impact on children is just as damaging. A nine-month-old who smiles at a stranger in a park is not flirting. A two-year-old who bites his friend in anger is not a bully. A three-year-old who throws a tantrum when she does not get what she wants is not naughty. A four-year-old who tells his peers what to do is not bossy. Mislabeling children's actions because of our own misunderstandings carries weighty repercussions, and as we learn to view childhood as a separate culture, we will also develop new language to more accurately describe the behaviors we see.

In the months following my escalator epiphany in Japan, I began to wonder what it would mean for the field of early childhood education if we reframed the way we thought about childhood. Rather than looking at children's early years as the first stop on a continuous railroad track of a human life, what if we started to think of childhood as a completely separate track? What if we viewed children as inhabiting a separate culture from adults? How would that altered perspective change our interactions? How would it shape our interpretations? No longer could we use the lens of adulthood to judge the behavior of children. We would have to enter the world of children to understand their behaviors, and align our responses accordingly.

Alison Gopnik reflects that "children aren't just defective adults, primitive grown-ups gradually attaining our perfection and complexity. Instead, children and adults are different forms of *Homo sapiens*. They have very different, though equally complex and powerful, minds, brains, and forms of consciousness, designed to serve different evolutionary functions" (2009, 9). In the way that Germans are not simply Americans in another location, children are not little adults. They don't behave based on the same worldview. They operate within a culture entirely distinct and separate from adults, and therefore, we must develop a framework for understanding children in a way that respects them and their unique culture. Looking at childhood in this way holds incredible potential for transformative care. I believe that learning to see childhood in this new way can make our work more effective, integrated, and sound.

The Day My Three-Year-Old Brought Home a Condom

My young son is always walking with his eyes searching the ground for hidden treasures (read: other people's discarded junk). When he was three, he had a particular liking for tags, tickets, and small pieces of packaging plastic. Price tags from toys, expired bus tickets, and the cloth tags cut out of the inside of T-shirts were the items overflowing from his treasure box at home. On a long walk one Sunday afternoon, my son had amassed a sizable collection of treasures along with procuring a small box to put them all in. He was showing off his treasures to his sisters on a crowded train while riding home: a broken piece of a tail light, assorted sticks, the plastic lid from a gum container, and a piece of very sparkly blue foil. My daughter asked to examine the contents. "You found a jam packet!" she exclaimed with enthusiasm, holding the sparkly blue foil package up so all members of the family could get a good look. Until this point I had not given the treasure a second thought, but the idea of a lonely jam packet lying on the ground waiting for rescue sounded odd. I took a second look to discover that it was not a jam packet. Nor was it simply a sparkly piece of blue foil. Or a price tag. No, what my son had found on that glorious fall morning was an unopened (thank goodness!) condom.

This moment is exactly why we need an appropriate cultural lens to bridge the divide between adults and children. In the culture of adulthood, condoms are connected to one thing: sex. But to view my son's treasure as a sex-related object would be to misunderstand its significance. To him, it was a shiny piece of foil. Better yet, it was a circular piece of plastic attached to a shiny piece of foil. It was the envy of tag-loving, plastic-collecting three-year-olds everywhere! But we were on a crowded train, and the children were holding up the condom in plain view of everyone around us, and I could only imagine what everyone else thought. If I had responded to my son's treasure with the awkwardness and humor that was the knee-jerk reaction of my adult culture, he would have been confused and embarrassed. Instead, I was able to align my response with his cultural awareness of the condom and simply say, "Would you put all your treasures back in your box so they don't get lost before we get off the train?"

An Invitation

In calling for a significant shift in our practice, *Discovering the Culture of Childhood* offers a new look at early childhood. The book has the power to transform the language that early childhood thinkers and practitioners use in thinking about and talking with young children. We can cease deriding the "terrible twos," disparaging the "naughty" children in our care, or being perplexed by the children who are "trying to make us angry" with their defiance. Instead, we can begin looking for the beliefs and assumptions of the culture behind a child's behavior. We can ask questions about cultural motivation in order to determine our course of action rather than focusing solely on a child's observable behaviors.

I invite you, readers, to imagine something new. Each day, as early childhood educators, we journey deep into the land of childhood. We are invited to leave our adult concerns and worries behind and don the hat of a storyteller, artist, puppeteer, or peacemaker. We make this journey because we desire to change and to be changed. But we've misunderstood the journey: in the past, we have come as tourists instead of culturally sensitive outsiders. We have formed judgments about children's behavior instead of allowing our surprise to push us toward understanding. We have arrived with assumptions, biases, and labels that may work in the adult world but do not apply to children.

What we don't realize is that the land of childhood is marvelously whole before we arrive. Within their world, children's behavior has logic and meaning. If we dare to encounter childhood through the eyes of the children in our care, equipped with the tools of curious outsiders, we will move toward a fuller understanding of the internal workings and logic of children. We have an invitation to notice the *surprise* that happens when the culture of adulthood and the culture of childhood meet.

Whether you are beginning this journey with children for the first time, or you've made this trip thousands of times, this book will shift your experience. As we join children in play, conflict resolution, forging new friendships, imagination, and finding a sense of belonging, we will discover the culture of childhood. What does it mean when children refuse to share? Why do children pretend to play with guns? What about children who exclude one another? From a diverse set of disciplines, we can embrace a culturally sound interpretation of childhood.

This book will present childhood in a new way. In chapter 1, we examine the significance of culture—what it is, who defines it, how it has been understood throughout history, and why it matters. Then, in chapters 2 through 6, we will look at childhood in the way that a cultural scientist (or anthropologist) would try to learn about a new group of people. Anthropologists look for certain elements that are present across cultures—social structure, language, beliefs, artistic expression, and economic systems. We will devote a chapter to each of these same pillars of culture in childhood, seeking to understand the implications of a culture of childhood for the care we provide. Included at the end of these chapters, you will find the voices of practitioners in the field of ECE, sharing their stories of working with children in culturally relevant ways.

Recognizing our adult cultural assumptions and biases is extremely difficult in isolation, and my hope is that this book will be used collaboratively between groups of educators seeking a new lens for understanding the behavior of young children. I have included a group discussion guide at the end of the book that you can use independently or with others, and hopefully this will extend the conversation beyond what I have written here. I invite you to reach out and interact with me about the book by visiting my website, emilyplank.com. There you will find resources for further study, my regular blog where I share stories and insights about childhood, and links for contacting me with questions or to invite me to video conference with your study group about this book.

Before You Embark

As you begin, I offer a few words of clarification to aid you in your journey. When I share factual stories, I have changed the names of children and adults in order to protect the identities of everyone involved. I use male and female pronouns interchangeably throughout the book because this makes the narrative easier to read than constantly relying on "him or her" or using the plural "children." I am aware that in following this style of reference, I risk communicating gender bias, both in the ways I attribute a story to either male or female, as well as in appearing to adhere to a gender binary. To be clear, this is not my intention, and whenever possible, I strive to write with inclusive, unbiased language.

The words we use to talk about professionals in the field of early childhood education can be extremely problematic. I use several words interchangeably when I'm talking about the adults who care for young children. I primarily rely on the terms *caregivers* and *early childhood educators* in reference to direct-care professionals such as classroom teachers, assistants, and family child care providers, and the term *early childhood professionals* when I am referring to the broader community in the field of early childhood education who do not necessarily work directly with young children, for example, consultants, legislators, resource personnel, and child care agency staff. Occasionally, I also use the terms *educator, teacher,* or *practitioner* when talking about direct-care professionals, and always my intention is to speak with utmost respect for those who are doing this incredibly critical work.

One final clarifying note before we all fasten our seatbelts and forge ahead into the world that awaits: *Discovering the Culture of Childhood* will be relevant for educators working with families whose cultural background is different from their own, but the primary focus of this book is the broad cultural categories of *adult* and *child* that exist wherever an age difference is present.

In approaching childhood as a distinct culture, we also have an opportunity to reflect on our own ways of understanding the world. As G. K. Chesterton asserted, "The whole object of travel is not to set foot on foreign land; it is at last to set foot on one's own country as a foreign land." It is my hope that this book will inspire dialogue and critical reflection that will lead to transformation among early childhood professionals with regards to the culture of adults and children: let us prepare to be changed.

CHAPTER ONE

"It's a Good Thing You're Fat!"
Why Culture Matters

"Waking up is a process. In the morning it is quite a different process for different people. Some of us wake up with a start and are wide awake for the rest of the day. They are lucky. Others have to do it stage by stage, cup of coffee by cup of coffee. What counts is that we don't go back to bed again."

—Brother David Steindl-Rast

SEVERAL YEARS AGO, MY PARTNER and I traveled to Thailand to celebrate our ten-year wedding anniversary. We had always dreamed of swimming in the magical turquoise water and eating authentic pad thai from the street vendors in Bangkok, and we were lucky enough to see our dream realized.

We embarked on our first snorkeling outing one morning at dawn in a small long-tail boat on the island of Koh Phi Phi Don. Our captain found a beautiful place for us to swim, and I eagerly jumped into the warm water of the Andaman Sea. I floated on the surface above bright rippling coral, an eight-legged sea star the size of a large pizza, giant black and white sea urchins with sharp spikes reaching high in the filtered sunlight, and a stealthy ray moving nearly undetected across the seafloor. I was so occupied with the bright, colorful, and diverse life below me that I failed to notice my proximity to our stationary boat.

As I brought my arm up and over my shoulder—*BAM!*—I swam right into the rudder.

My arm radiated with pain as I fumbled for the source of my injury. When I realized that I had floated right into our anchored boat, I felt too foolish to draw attention to my misery. Fortunately, in the end, the only injury I incurred, besides the wound to my pride, was a black-and-blue bruise the size of a peach.

Later in the week, my partner and I were sitting in a small café enjoying an exquisite papaya salad and Thai iced tea. I was wearing a sleeveless shirt and the bruise stood out prominently on my right arm. Our server came to check in, and we began talking with him about our vacation and the wonderful time we were having.

After a few pleasantries, he noticed my bruise and commented, "Ouch! That looks painful. What did you do?" I responded, "I ran into the rudder of our boat while I was snorkeling. Ha! At least the boat wasn't running." His follow-up comment startled me: "It's a good thing you're fat. Otherwise, you would have really been hurt!"

The Complete Behavior Guidebook

Enter an imaginary world with me for a moment. Sitting alongside both my partner and me at the café table, and tucked neatly into the apron pocket of our waiter, are copies of a book called *The Complete Behavior Guidebook*. Now this book is imaginary, but it will serve as a useful metaphor as we explore the nature of culture. It spells out the particularities of appropriate behavior in any possible situation. It tells us what to say to strangers, how to act at the meal table, appropriate ways to cross the street, the appropriate speaking volume when riding the bus, how to respond when you find out you failed at a task—basically, the recommended reaction to any conceivable social scenario.

My guidebook to behavior, written over my years of growing up in Los Angeles, does not include the phrase "It's a good thing you're fat" as an appropriate thing to say to a stranger. In fact, if you were to look for that phrase in the Emily Plank edition, you would find

it under the section titled "Absolutely Prohibited Topics of Conversation with Strangers or Friends," or possibly the section called "What
to Say as a Restaurant Server if You Don't Want to Get a Tip," or even
"Good Phrases to Guarantee a Fistfight." This phrase would appear
alongside other forbidden conversation starters with strangers, such as
"How much money do you make?" or "Tell me what you think of the
proposed tax increases on the middle class."

The more difficult thing is that *each of us carries a different guidebook.* Most of the people in my immediate community carry one that
looks very similar to mine, with nuances that depend on year of birth,
family structure, racial background, ability level, and socioeconomic
class. But, for the most part, the culture in which I claim membership behaves in much the same way as I do. My Thai waiter, however,
carries an entirely different guidebook full of different social expectations. His guidebook includes greeting people with a slight bow and
palms pressed together instead of a handshake, removing shoes to enter
a residence, and—apparently—designating a different set of "taboo"
conversation topics.

Successful cross-cultural interactions don't require that we first
become fluent in the guidebooks of other people, but merely that we
remain aware of our different guidebooks, and let that awareness drive
our interactions. In that restaurant in Thailand, I didn't grow angry at
a "rude" waiter, but instead wondered with surprise at the motivations
behind his words. I was free to embrace his comment as an expression
of empathy for my pain and as a kind gesture of concern. Cross-cultural
success, indeed!

The Contents of Our Guidebooks

Let us continue to imagine culture as a guidebook. If we were to open
our guidebooks and skim the table of contents, we would find the broad
categories of our beliefs and behaviors. There would be chapters on
acceptable parenting practices, managing anger, personal hygiene, and
even appropriate dress in inclement weather. Every one of our human
behaviors is learned over our lifetimes and shaped by the particular

environments in which we grew up. Not a single behavior is exempt from cultural nuances. Even our biological needs have a cultural element. While every human culture shares the same biological needs, each culture responds differently to those needs. In some cultures, for example, burping is a sign that the meal just finished was delicious and the burp is a compliment to the chef, while in others, burping in public is offensive and rude.

Recently, I talked with a Swiss friend about doing laundry. I confessed that laundry is one of the most challenging household responsibilities for me. It is a rare day indeed that I don't have piles of clean laundry around my house, waiting to be folded, put away, or worn. She agreed that laundry was a difficult task in her home but that the washing and drying were not problems—it was the ironing that overwhelmed her. *The ironing?* In my home, ironing is done irregularly for professional attire. If, for example, the T-shirt my son chooses for the day looks as if it sat in a ball at the bottom of my laundry basket for a week waiting to be folded, it probably did, and I rely on gravity to help the wrinkles fall out. My friend told me that with the sole exception of undergarments, *everyone* in Switzerland irons *everything*: T-shirts, jeans, sweaters, bedsheets, towels—everything. She even irons all of her baby's onesies and soft cotton pants, though she admitted that was a bit excessive, even by Swiss standards. In Switzerland, my standards for ironing would be considered outright slovenly. And just think: if I had grown up in Switzerland as a child of Swiss parents, I might expect an American such as myself also to iron all my clothes.

This is culture. Based on the behavioral habits and customs of those around us during our growing years, we all develop a system of beliefs and behaviors. Our beliefs motivate our actions, though they are often unquestioned until we interact with someone from a different culture.

A Short History of Cultural Anthropology

To explore childhood as a unique culture, we must first understand the way cultures are studied. The study of human nature is called *anthropology,* and the scientists who conduct this study are *anthropologists.* Anthropologists study everything from fossils and architecture to the consumption of fast food and the way we construct our text messages in order to discover the particularities of different groups of people, past and present. This field of study has changed dramatically over the past two centuries. Early anthropologists believed in a continuum model of social development, asserting that societies existed on a spectrum from "savage" to "civilized." Some ethnic groups, then, were said to be more advanced and civilized than others. Anthropologists believed it was their mission to live among "primitive" peoples to study and document their way of life before it evolved into a higher form. There was an element of urgency to their work because they believed that "less civilized" peoples would enable scientists to discover the elementary structures of advanced society, before those civilizations inevitably became more modern.

Throughout the 1800s and early 1900s, this model dominated the field of anthropology. Cultures were thought to fall along a continuum with Western Europe situated at the most "civilized" end of that continuum. A nineteenth-century anthropologist, Lewis Henry Morgan, first named these stages of development in 1877: lower savagery, middle savagery, upper savagery, lower barbarism, middle barbarism, upper barbarism, and civilization (Rogoff 2003, 19).

In the 1930s another scientist, Franz Boas, flatly rejected the continuum model of anthropology. What if culture were not a mark of progress, not a state of being that you could attain in varying degrees, and, most important, not a system for evaluating human beings? What if Western Europe were not the pinnacle of civilization? Instead, what if the term *culture* simply described how any group of people thought and behaved? In this way, culture was something belonging to everyone. Boas suggested that culture shaped every action and every thought, serving as the motivator of all behavior and the filter by which we evaluated the behavior of others. He believed that civilization was not absolute but relative. His proposal was revolutionary: culture is not the prize of the powerful; rather, it is a reality that shapes the existence of every human being on our planet. Boas's new metaphor for understanding culture was a "lens": each person had a cultural "lens" that allowed him to "see" the world in a unique way. Boas is responsible for training an entire generation of influential thinkers and researchers, and he is considered the father of modern cultural anthropology (Monanghan and Just 2000, 36–39).

Under Morgan's continuum model, people who hold season tickets to the New York Philharmonic and dine before the show on escargot and champagne are clearly more civilized—more "cultured"—than people who watch old soap opera reruns on their DVRs while drinking boxed wine and eating Doritos. Boas argued fervently against this scientific racism, championing a new way to understand human and social development.

Adults Are Not the Pinnacle

The story of anthropology's beginning is a great description of where we find ourselves in the early childhood community today. Modern society continues to support and perpetuate an idea of childhood that places the young on a continuum. Instead of calling this continuum "degrees of civilization," as Lewis Henry Morgan did, I would like to suggest that we call our model of childhood development "degrees of adulthood." We measure children according to the level of "adultness" they have attained: Can they sleep through the night? Walk and eat on their own? Speak in sentences? Sit still for music time?

Much like early anthropologists, parents and early childhood educators eagerly observe their subjects for signs that they are moving from one level of development to the next. Infants are taken regularly to the doctor for well-child visits where they are given developmental screenings to make sure they are "on track" even though children often develop at different rates. When my first child was born, she took *forever* to sleep through the night. As a new, sleep-deprived mother, I could not wait until the two of us would stop meeting for our middle-of-the-night rendezvous. At first, friends reassured me that six weeks would be a turning point. After the six-week mark passed, they told me that three months would certainly be the magic moment. When three months turned into four, and then five, they agreed that she needed to start solid foods to stay full through the night. I asked my pediatrician and every new parent I could about the secrets. "What can I do to help her sleep through the night?" Everyone had their ideas, and I tried them all. Then one day, as she neared the end of her first year of life and without any big fanfare, she just figured it out.

There is nothing wrong with knowing the benchmarks of development and preparing for the next phase of a child's life. When we know generally what to expect, we can be prepared with appropriate tools and methods for accompanying children on their journey, and we can support children who need assistance to move from one milestone to the next. Many children do learn to speak, gain control of their bladders, and find success in eating soup from a spoon, and as caregivers, if we know where they are and where they are going, we can support them in these efforts.

The challenge of this model is that it focuses on children's perceived deficiencies. Under the development model, my daughter was a human being who could not sleep through the night uninterrupted instead of a human being who was really good at eating when she was hungry. These subtle shifts in thinking have tremendous implications for our work with young children. I once worked with a child who seemed extremely introverted. She often spent whole days in my program by herself, reading in the book corner. I obsessed over this child, concerned that her needs were not being met in my program. After consulting with the family, I connected with support services in the area and secured a developmental screening. In the meantime, I talked with a trusted colleague, concerned that I wasn't doing all I could to help nurture this child. My colleague agreed that screenings and outside evaluations were important, but also challenged me to change my perspective. What if I began to look for the child's strengths? For the things she was really good at doing? Would I see a child who was thoughtful and deliberate? A child with an incredible attention span?

A child who was an eager observer? My colleague's words gave me new eyes to appreciate the abilities of this child, and as I fine-tuned my environment to meet her unique needs, it was with her competencies at the forefront of my mind.

As a community of early childhood professionals, we depend on developmental measures to help us identify children who might need additional support services and to help us as we plan appropriately for the children in our care. At the same time, when we rely too heavily on developmental models of human development for understanding childhood, we can fall into a trap of seeing children only for the future adults they will become. We begin to anticipate the child's next stages so intensely that we miss the capabilities of the child in the present moment. "She's getting so close to walking." "I heard him put three words together. He's almost talking in sentences!" "Before you know it, he'll be eating table foods!" When the only model we have for understanding childhood is a continuum of development, childhood is always measured against adulthood.

Let's suspend present thinking for a moment and entertain a different reality entirely. How would human development look different if we reversed the continuum? For while we gain skills as we age, we also lose them. Imagine what this might look like. Babies have incredible physical flexibility that enables them to spend time sucking on their hands and feet. And while we might wonder how long it will be before they can sit or roll onto their stomachs independently, this period of time while they lie on their backs sucking on their feet is critical to their developing spatial sense. They are testing the limitations of their own bodies, finding out where they begin and where they end. Babies are as good as they need to be at problem solving the physical boundaries of their bodies. Instead of limited mobility, they have supernatural flexibility that serves exactly the purpose it needs to (Forbes 2004, 15).

Toddlers are excellent at repetitive, impromptu, whole-group activities. Often in my program as I was setting dishes out at mealtimes, the toddlers would begin banging their hands on the table. One by one, all would join in, until they were all pounding their hands on the table. I was not a big fan of this activity and frequently chose to interrupt it. But when I explored their experience from inside the culture of childhood, I discovered something incredible. In the toddler years, children are discovering the power of a peer group, but they lack the wording to enter, create, or sustain the lengthy play scripts of their older peers, which is why toddlers are known for the developmental phase of parallel play—they play alongside, but not necessarily *with*, each other. This table game, however, is different. In constructing such a simple refrain of hand pounding, they are inventing something they can all do together, something anyone can join in at any time. In doing it day after day, they are creating multiple opportunities to play together and experience peer culture, not to mention the power of creating such loud sounds together and eliciting such a predictable reaction from me (Corsaro 2011). Toddlers frequently create these kinds of simple scripts that they repeat over and over. We will look more closely at this example in chapter 2, but these toddlers are engaged in something far richer than parallel play; it is an example of highly sophisticated social interaction. Instead of focusing on the limited or repetitive nature of their play, we can marvel at their capacity to create play that resonates within their peer group.

In addition to their physical flexibility and capacity for repetitive, group-oriented games, children possess a multitude of abilities that perfectly situate them for their present experiences. Unfortunately, when we focus on the degrees to which they have progressed toward adulthood, we miss the gifts they bring in the present.

We measure children's development against ourselves, and implicit in their maturation is the notion that they are "less than" they will be when they grow up. We misread their behavioral cues and fail to appreciate the unique perspective they bring to every situation. This model perpetuates the same biases and misunderstandings that arose when anthropologists tried to place human races on a scale from savage to civil. We even have popular parenting books that define toddlers as "charming chimp-children" and "knee-high Neanderthals," and with small exception, few stop to question the bias that exists within that framework (Karp 2008).

Seeing Children Differently

I believe the field of early childhood education must reframe our understanding of human beings so that middle-aged adulthood no longer resides at the pinnacle of a mythical developmental pyramid. Just as Franz Boas leveled the field by eliminating labels like "barbaric" and "savage" and asserting that all groups had their own culture, the time has come to stop judging the culture of childhood by the culture of adulthood. Children are members of a separate culture and deserve recognition that they possess their own *Complete Behavior Guidebook*. Furthermore, they deserve the respect of adults and interactions that reflect culturally appropriate methods.

Much of the evidence for Boas's new model in anthropology came from the scientists who lived and worked among the groups they were studying. These ethnographers studied groups of people considered to be simpleminded and unsophisticated, and discovered high levels of complexity and structure. In trying to understand how childhood is a distinct culture, we adults who live and work among children are like ethnographers, seeking to understand them in their own cultural context. Furthermore, we oppose systems that try to impose culturally irrelevant patterns of thinking and behavior on children. Children are not primitive adults, and they are not incomplete human beings; they are whole human beings who deserve to be understood and respected.

Boas and other scientists who followed believed they were establishing a system that would counter racism and ethnocentrism that grows out of sentiments of superiority. I understand my unique cultural orientation as one that was created by my geography, history, and community rather than perpetuating an understanding that ignores the existence of any other worldview, or uses my own worldview as the measure of rightness. I see others as products of their culture, embedded in a way of being that is different from my own.

A New Model for Childhood

In my travels outside the United States, I have been embarrassed many times because I did not understand specific cultural expectations. I remember sipping my wine once at dinner before the other guests had lifted their glasses and toasted one another. In that country, I had committed a disrespectful faux pas. In another country, my children talked too loudly on the metro, not realizing that the expectation for noise in public spaces was very different from what we have in the United States. The stakes have never been high enough in my personal cross-cultural encounters to cause anything more than embarrassment or discomfort, but cultural misunderstandings have led to countless catastrophes, including wars between empires, genocide, colonialism, and long-standing impasses between nations. Such misunderstandings continue to fuel economic disparities, violence, and racism.

In the same way that cross-cultural breakdowns between countries can cause everything from minor mishaps to more egregious atrocities, these misunderstandings between adults and children can range from minor to catastrophic. These misunderstandings help us, for example, view a toddler having a tantrum as being naughty rather than considering the needs she is trying to communicate. In the chapters that follow, we will explore the implications of these misunderstandings in more detail. For now, I want to define the three main areas in which I feel this new look at childhood holds the potential to transform our practice.

1. The awareness that children inhabit a distinct culture demands that we truly appreciate children for who they are now.

In working with young children, we have a tendency to focus on who children will grow up to be rather than focusing on and respecting their present needs. As Priscilla Alderson argues, we fail to see children as "human beings" and instead see them as "human becomings" (2008, 26). Consider how often parents or educators are advised to ignore the unwanted behaviors of young children because they are "just a phase." The disheartening implication of that advice is the idea that the undesirable qualities of childhood do not deserve attention because those qualities will be short-lived; if we can just endure the present annoyances a little longer, then they will go away. And while I feel like perspective is helpful in the midst of very difficult behavior (the awareness that children are in a "phase" of development might be the lifeline that a parent needs to survive one more wakeful night with a child who isn't sleeping), this perspective encourages providers to selectively ignore the behaviors of children that they find undesirable. Children will eventually stop pounding on the table at mealtime, eating their food with their hands, or blowing bubbles in their milk, so instead of *tuning in* to what those behaviors mean in the moment and addressing them in ways that would be meaningful for everyone involved, we *tune out* and wait for the undesirable behavior to pass. Can you imagine if someone did the same thing to you when you were acting undesirably?

Focusing so intensely on the future instead of rooting ourselves in the present influences our behavior. We evaluate childhood social interactions as if the children in our care were potential grown-ups, rather than looking for the meaning of their behavior from within their culture, expecting two-year-olds to willingly share their toys or four-year-olds to include everyone in their play. We orchestrate art projects with defined end products. We expect behavior of our children in anticipation of what they will be expected to do next, like requiring four-year-olds to sit for circle time because they will be expected to do this in kindergarten. And we discipline their mistakes without regard for the impact of those behavior modification techniques on their feelings of love and belonging: "You cannot hit. Go sit in time-out for five minutes."

When childhood is one step on the journey toward adulthood, everything we do with children is measured in terms of the strides made on that path. As Steven Mintz observes, "American culture—oriented toward mastery and control—views childhood as a 'project,' in which the young must develop the skills, knowledge, and character traits necessary for adulthood success" (2004, 383). Viewing children as members of a distinct culture allows us to step off the assembly line of human development and pay attention to what children need in the present.

2. Failing to see childhood as a unique culture leads to the wrong conclusions about childhood behaviors.

When I use the wrong cultural lens to evaluate the behavior of my Thai waiter who referred to me as fat, I become offended by his rudeness rather than appreciative of his empathy over an injury that could have been much worse. When my Swiss neighbors use the wrong lens to evaluate my laundry habits, they see me as lazy or unkempt rather than a busy adult successfully keeping my laundry clean. Likewise, when I use my adult lens to evaluate the behaviors of young children, I am likely to misunderstand their meaning. I am likely to view the three-year-old who kicks her friend as naughty rather than discovering that she lacks the tools to enter play. I am likely to misread the repeated spoon dropping during mealtimes of a nine-month-old as mischievous or "trying to make me mad" rather than an attempt at the give-and-take of conversation. I am likely to react rather than understand, to lecture rather than listen, to coerce rather than cooperate, and demand rather than ask.

The reasons for a child's behavior matter, and the way we assess the child's motivation affects the ways we respond. I didn't storm out of the restaurant in Thailand because the waiter had "insulted" me. I understood that the rules were different. In the same way, we need to question our responses to children's actions as coming from their own unique culture.

Imagine eighteen-month-old Samuel, boisterous, gregarious, and exploring everything with an insatiable quest for understanding. One day when he arrives at child care, he finds that his provider, Joyce, has left the television remote control conveniently within his reach. What luck! Joyce is busy feeding one of the other children, but when Samuel heads for the glorious button-filled wand, Joyce calls from across the room and tells him to stop. *Really? Stop? Have you* seen *the remote control? This thing is amazing!* Samuel looks Joyce square in the eye, smiles, and touches the forbidden remote control anyway.

From within adult culture, this kind of behavior is clearly defiant. If my neighbor asked to borrow my car and I said no, but she smiled at me with her eyes locked on mine, took the keys, and drove away anyway, I would be outraged and flabbergasted. I would assume she was trying to make me angry, and that belief would guide my behavior. I would draw a careful line between the neighbor and myself, protecting my possessions as well as my emotions from someone so disrespectful and malicious.

With toddlers, the stakes are different, but the responses are similar. Joyce might feel the need to punish Samuel's misbehavior with a time-out or a harsh "no" so he learns a lesson. She might take his behavior personally, allowing it to engender feelings of frustration and irritability. But fortunately, there is a different explanation for the so-called defiant behavior. Behind the scenes, Samuel is learning that different people can have different opinions, and that fact is striking to him. He smiles and persists with what he was doing, not because he has some malicious purpose behind his noncompliance, but because he simply cannot believe that two people hold different opinions (Gopnik, Meltzoff, and Kuhl 2001, 32). He smiles because he is wonderstruck. He smiles because he is connecting with the human who is trying to stop him from touching the remote control. He doesn't really care about the remote control as much as he is playing with the beginnings of this newfound knowledge. For early childhood educators, information like this is powerful because it shapes our response. Instead of a time-out to teach Samuel not to misbehave, Joyce can gently remove the remote control and set it out of reach. She is free to remain calm and kind, and respectful of his desire while she guides his behavior. "You really like this. I can't let you have it, so I'll put it up on this shelf." Joyce still sets the limit: Samuel cannot touch the remote control. But Joyce doesn't take it personally, and she understands the need to construct an environment that supports his exploration. She isn't surprised when Samuel is attracted to the remote control, and she is even less surprised when her "no" is met with curious and playful resistance, but Joyce appreciates the back-and-forth as a sign of competent empathetic awareness, and that appreciation transforms her ability to care for Samuel.

3. Viewing childhood as a distinct culture shifts the nature of adult-child relationships from one of hierarchy and power to one of mutual respect.

Modern society, though it might never verbalize it as such, unconsciously accepts children's developmental differences as a sort of disability. Influential theorists like Sigmund Freud and Jean Piaget operated with assumptions that children were incomplete human beings, and their ways of making sense of the world were incomplete. From a sociological perspective, Allison James and Alan Prout observe that "rationality is the universal mark of adulthood with childhood representing the period of apprenticeship for its development. Childhood is therefore important to study as a presocial period of difference, a biologically determined stage on the path to full human status i.e., adulthood" (2015, 9). As early childhood educators, we are taught to watch for clues about budding growth. Children, as evidenced by their biology, their cognitive fortitude, their nuanced emotional understandings, and even their play abilities, should be understood in terms of *development*. With a developmental theory of childhood, four- and five-year-olds—by their ability to engage skillfully in cooperative play—are more socially *developed* than toddlers. For the most part, the developmental time lines offered throughout the twentieth century by Jean Piaget, Sigmund Freud, Erik Erikson, and others were adopted unquestioningly by educators and parenting experts around the world.

Alison Gopnik, herself a developmental psychologist, takes issue with the claims made within her own field by these influential theorists. According to Gopnik, advances in science debunk many of the claims made by Piaget and others, but the field has yet to catch up to more modern scientific discoveries about the incredible capabilities of young children. Gopnik points out in *The Philosophical Baby* that these outdated beliefs are wrong but persist regardless (2009, 20). The marks we see as signs of childhood immaturity are actually highly sophisticated tools for learning and growth. Play is a highly complex tool for developing a worldview, imaginary friends offer a sophisticated alternative reality that allows children to test the laws of behavior, and children's uninhibited, "unfocused" attention is precisely what allows them to learn so quickly and rapidly. We don't understand that the ways children interact with the world have developmental purposes of their own, necessary and complete as they are.

Many people cringe at the thought of spending an afternoon with a toddler (though I suspect the "cringers" would be a much smaller percentage of those reading this book than a typical sampling of the adult population). Why do we shudder at the thought of spending a day with two-year-olds? After all, they are creative, passionate, curious, loving, and energetic. The reasons we cringe are partly due to the reputation of the "terrible twos," a phrase coined in the 1920s by a scientist named Arnold Gesell. Gesell was the first to study this period of human development in an attempt to understand the stubbornness for which toddlers have become known (Mintz 2004, 219). Some in education have tried to reclaim the age, referring to children as experiencing the "terrific twos," while others have found ways to label subsequent phases of development in similarly disparaging ways. Labels such as the "trying threes" and "ferocious fours" have grown more commonplace, even in early childhood education circles. I have frequently overheard conversations between parents along the lines of, "You think the twos are hard? Just wait for the threes!" Even though many of our understandings about childhood have changed, and we know that what many adults perceive as a toddler's inflexibility is actually evidence of developing autonomy and empathy, popular notions of toddlers as inflexible, self-centered monsters pervade our social consciousness (Gopnik, Meltzoff, and Kuhl 2001, 38–39).

Children are not imperfect humans, but they are imperfect adults. As long as we evaluate children by how well they do adult tasks, the observation often attributed to Albert Einstein rings true: "Everybody is a genius. But if you judge a fish by its ability to climb a tree, it will spend its whole life believing it is stupid." We must learn to stop evaluating children by how well they do adult tasks. If we never change our rubric, they will always appear deficient. Shifting our understanding to appreciate children as members of a separate culture permits us to do just that.

Viewing childhood as a culture does not release adults from their responsibility of caring for children; adults will still determine many pieces of a child's life, such as setting the daily schedule, deciding the menu, maintaining the environment, and intervening on issues of safety and security. A cultural lens model of childhood offers a wholly new style that embraces children not as imperfect adults or partially formed human beings, but as complete and distinct individuals. In the same way that Franz Boas believed his cultural lens model had the power to undo racism, it is my belief that applying this cultural lens model to childhood holds a similar transformative power.

The Curious Case of Childhood as Culture

Andrew Solomon's book *Far from the Tree* describes the distinction between vertical and horizontal identities. According to Solomon, vertical identities are "attributes and values [that] are passed down from parent to child across the generations not only through strands of DNA, but also through shared cultural norms" (2013, 2). Characteristics such as ethnicity, race, and language are typically part of a person's vertical identity. A horizontal identity, by contrast, is an "inherent or acquired trait that is foreign to [a person's] parents"; the person "must therefore acquire identity from a peer group" (2). Sexual orientation and ability are horizontal identities because children do not automatically share those with their parents, and often find the greatest support in their search for identity among a peer cohort.

Childhood is a kind of unique horizontal identity that can exist almost unnoticed within society. I think it is so hard to recognize because, while we were all children at one time, our move from childhood to adulthood happened so gradually it was almost imperceptible.

The move from child to adult comes with well-known challenges such as body changes, awkward middle school dances, first relationships, and teenage angst that most of us wouldn't be eager to repeat, but aside from these landmarks, the move is subtle in the same way that the gray sky of early dawn gives way to full daylight.

Childhood is distinct from all other cultural memberships. We were all children at one time, and we all moved into the culture of adulthood simply as a function of how many years we've been alive. Portuguese expatriates do not instantly become culturally American after living in the United States for a certain period of time. The child with hearing loss who receives a cochlear implant does not by her new-found hearing gain membership in the hearing culture. But children, sometime between birth and the recognized age of maturity, move from the culture of childhood into the culture of adulthood—whether they like it or not.

As we move more deeply into a discussion of the ways in which childhood culture is shaped and defined, we will have to overcome our own roadblocks to transforming our vision. Considering childhood from a radically new perspective may throw us off balance and challenge our status quo. We may be disoriented to learn the ways in which our own belief systems perpetuate discrimination against children. We may experience a sort of culture shock when we reflect on our own assumptions. This work may be unsettling, but in that process, there are many opportunities for growth. In suspending our own adult perspectives, we are challenged to grow individually and within our communities.

CHAPTER TWO

"Poison Meat Eaters"
The Social Lives of Children

"The child is portrayed, like the laboratory rat, as being at the mercy of external stimuli: passive and conforming. Lost in a social maze it is the adult who offers directions. The child, like the rat, responds accordingly and is finally rewarded by becoming 'social,' by becoming adult."

—Allison James and Alan Prout

"Simone, this is the best birthday ever, and you made it that way. It would not be this special without you. I feel very loved."

—Tekoa on her sixth birthday,
to her four-year-old sister

ARE CHILDREN INHERENTLY SOCIAL? Most people would say that yes, human beings are born social creatures. Infancy thrives in the context of a community that provides more than just shelter, food, and basic needs. The call and response that unfolds between babies and caregivers is the fertile ground for this thriving. A baby cries and she is fed. She squirms and her diaper is changed. She locks her gaze with that of a loved one, and her adoring loved one returns the stare.

Babies are innately social.

Then, something happens toward the end of the first year of life that will morph and transform in shape, but remain a constant drive through the early years. The perceived helpless dependence of early infancy gives way to a drive for independence. The child's desire to "do it myself!" eclipses the previously unquestioned adult job of buckling a car seat or zipping up a coat. The child's desire to test physical limits leads to climbing, running, and jumping that suddenly bring questions of safety to the forefront. In anger, the child might bite or hit or kick. The child might take toys without asking, or exclude peers from play, or retain dictator-like control of a play script.

Has something changed? Do children lose their sociability? Are their natural desires for social connection proof of *real* social structure, or is the culture of childhood a presocial space where children muddle along, clashing with peers until they can absorb the social teachings of their parents and caregivers? Anthropologist Enid Schildkrout observes that often "child culture is seen as a rehearsal for adult life and socialization consists of the processes through which, by one method or another, children are made to conform" (2002, 345). Many of our modern beliefs about young children testify to our deep belief in presocial children, similar to commonly held beliefs that children are egocentric, or that they don't know how to share, or that their friendships aren't authentic and deep.

The adult bias about children's social structure has two layers. First, adults believe that if any social structure does exist, it consists of negative interactions between children: children hit one another, take toys, push, bite, and exclude each other from play. Second, when children do have successful peer interactions, it is because of the hard work of dedicated parents and child care professionals—they don't learn to be social on their own.

In large part, these biases are rooted in a developmental understanding of childhood, fed by influential theorists such as Piaget and Freud, but also shaped through lesser-known voices such as that of American sociologist Mildred Parten. In 1932 Parten published her stages of play theory, which said that children move sequentially through social play stages: solitary play, onlooker play, parallel play, associative play, and cooperative play. Similar to the developmental time lines of her contemporaries, Parten's theory was rooted in the mind-set that children's development served as a useful rubric for measuring their progress toward adulthood. Older children "stuck" at the parallel play stage evidenced a biological or social lack, whereas toddlers were incapable of higher-level group interactions.

These developmental models are helpful in identifying the basic contours of childhood, but they have severely limited our interactions with young children, preventing us from seeing the social capacity young children possess. Modern training for early childhood educators describes solitary play as "the lowest level of social play" and parallel play as "a point of transition between the socially immature level of solitary play and the socially sophisticated level of genuine cooperation" (Hughes 2009, 102). And while it is true that children's social relationships will change over time, the practice of plotting childhood on a continuum undermines the concept of a unique culture of childhood. Abraham Maslow said famously, "I suppose it is tempting, if the only tool you have is a hammer, to treat everything as if it were a nail" (1966, 15–16). If all we expect of babies is eating, sleeping, and pooping, then we miss the rich social connections they are forming from birth. If all we expect for toddler peers is a kind of tense parallel existence, then we miss thousands of examples of highly sophisticated social interactions. If we expect that infants and toddlers are trapped in an egocentric phase of development, then we don't attend to the vast empathetic social connections they are making. If we believe that children in our care are antisocial by nature, then we work hard to "socialize" them to *share* or *be nice*.

The culture of adulthood sees the culture of childhood through this developmental paradigm, under which children are always measured by their proximity to the complete state of adulthood. As a counter to this, Ian Hutchby and Jo Moran-Ellis (2005) coined the phrase "competence paradigm," through which children are understood to be whole and complete human beings, worthy of study as active writers of their own stories rather than passive actors. The competence paradigm does not refute the idea that development happens, or even that it can be useful in constructing an appropriate early childhood setting. It simply asserts that children are—first and foremost—competent in their interactions and that our responsibility is to maintain a posture of curiosity as we approach childhood. Embracing childhood as a culture is an invitation to consider children from this paradigm of competency.

As we distance ourselves from the strict measurement of a developmental approach to childhood, we have to clarify our role as adults. Children are competent social actors, but adults still have a role in shaping children's social behavior. When children take toys from one another, hit or kick peers to try to get their way, or try to take toys home that belong at school, adults will (and should) intervene. But we are wrong to believe that children are egocentric, or that children are incapable of experiencing complex friendships. We are wrong to believe that children don't know how to share. We are wrong to believe that children are naturally selfish or antisocial. These beliefs influence the way we shape children's social behavior. If, instead, we begin from a place of competency, we look at childhood behaviors with new eyes. Norwegian scholar Gunvor Løkken notes in her work on toddler peer culture that examining children's social systems from the inside "should challenge any view that toddler relations are rare, short-lived and often aggressive, and as such continuously in need of adult or older children's support" (2000, 173).

A shift in our paradigm changes everything. Hutchby and Moran-Ellis say that in looking for the competencies, we find "a picture of childhood as a dynamic arena of social activity involving struggles for power, contested meanings and negotiated relationships, rather than the linear picture of development and maturation made popular by traditional sociology and developmental psychology" (2005, 10). The social structure of early childhood looks different from the social structure of adulthood, and to appreciate it and mine the significance of peer connections in early childhood, we're going to have to look from the inside.

Friendship in the Culture of Childhood

One of the most basic social categories is that of a friend, and it's a category that those of us in early childhood settings spend lots of time helping children understand. First of all, we use the word *friend* constantly—"Friends, let's come to the carpet for reading time!" "She shared a shovel with you. She's a friend." "Thank you, friends, for being so quiet for the story." Our vocabulary helps shape a child's growing notion of what it means to be a friend, but we often use *friend* as a noun when *children* would be equally suitable. "Let's leave for the park, friends/children." Applying *friend* to every child in every situation can ascribe motivation that was absent from the interaction, confusing the actual root of friendship.

In addition, we work hard to teach children the definition of a friend without stopping to inquire about their existing definition. Children have a strong concept of friendship that resembles but does not strictly imitate the definition of friendship used by adults. Children use several different definitions to understand friendship.

Friendship Is Public

When I was in elementary and middle school, everyone at our school wore "best friends" necklaces—single, delicate silver or gold hearts split in two with the words "best" and "friend" emblazoned on the separate halves. My best friend, Erin, and I were no exception. Because our mothers were friends, our friendship started when we were born, so it was only natural that we would wear these public professions of our friendship each day to school. In the years since middle school, we have laughed, grieved, carried each other through difficulties, and rejoiced in celebration with each other's significant life events. Our inside jokes and memories of all-night slumber parties or times when we got into trouble imbue our lives with meaning in a deep well of belonging.

Erin and I have been friends for my entire lifetime, but I no longer wear my "best friends" necklace. In fact, I no longer have it. I recently checked with Erin: she no longer has her necklace either. The public symbol of our friendship has lost its significance, not because the friendship is any less important but because the fabric of the friendship has transformed as we have grown. Allison James offers this definition of childhood friendship:

> It must be affirmed, confirmed and reaffirmed through social action. This explains how emphasis on "sameness" and conformity in children's social relationships—wearing the same clothes, eating the same food, liking the same football teams—works to mitigate the significance which any differences might have. It represents one visible demonstration of friendship, for it is through such public performances that children evaluate and acknowledge their friendship with one another: being friends must not only be experienced but be seen to be experienced (1993, 215).

Friendship between young children is more than knowing or feeling affection for someone; friendship is a public experience, seen and affirmed from the outside as much as any internal, cognitive belief. It is relating to someone in the moment through play.

Friends Have Shared Experiences

Shared experiences are a critical aspect of friendship that is important for all ages, not just children, but the types of experiences we engage in are different. As adults, Erin and I reflect on our long history of shared experiences. We reconnect through reflecting on points of intersection in our lives—what our children are up to, our love for literature and movies, and how our families are doing, but we don't actively create shared experiences as a means of feeling connected to one another. Our feelings of being connected reside in the common history we already have. Children don't draw from past shared experiences to define friendship; rather, they create their friendships as they engage in shared experiences in the present moment.

When I first opened my family child care program, I had three young children enrolled: a nine-month-old, a fourteen-month-old, and a seventeen-month-old. Each day at lunch, I would place the children in their booster seats at the table while I finished lunchtime preparations. Over a period of several weeks, the children developed a pattern that I did not appreciate. I set plastic plates in front of them as I moved between the kitchen and table bringing the food and drinks. One afternoon, the fourteen-month-old picked up her empty plate and pounded it on the table, accompanied by a loud "Ai!" She locked eyes with the older child nearby and smiled. In response, he picked up his plate and imitated her behavior. The two children pounded their plates in a back-and-forth manner two or three times before the youngest joined the routine. Soon, all three are pounding and "Ai"-ing in sync, growing louder and louder with each pound. They smiled and laughed. I remember being so perplexed. I was bothered by the noise and tried to stop the behavior. I took the plates away until they were ready for use, but the children pounded with their hands. I tried distracting them by singing songs, but they persisted. I tried speaking in a stern voice with raised eyebrows. "Let's use gentle hands," I said, but the children just smiled and kept on pounding. I was exhausted and exasperated; I lacked an adequate interpretation for the grand display of noise.

I had no idea that this event was the hallmark of friendship, adapted for the toddler peers. These children—despite their young age—already knew how to create a shared experience. I did not see it as an act of friendship. In the best moments, I named their actions as curiosity or joy, but in less favorable moments, I saw their actions as malicious, willful, and intended to make me angry. Now I see that these children were witnessing to their friendship, creating a common experience that, through its simplicity and repetition, each child could access. Reframing the memory in this way infuses it with such rich meaning and assigns competency to an act that used to seem meaningless and haphazard.

For children, the social category of "friends" is made up of those individuals who are actively engaged in a shared experience in the moment. In fact, asking children to explain their friendships results in answers that are related to some action: "He is my friend because he plays cars with me." "She is my friend because we build towers together."

Very often, when children talk about friends, they do not call to mind the same connotations adults use. Those who are actively engaged in creating shared experiences automatically belong to a category called "friend." Those outside the category are "not friends." Over time, children can internalize a feeling about a particular child, and "he's not my friend" might point toward a larger conflict beyond simply not playing together. Often, however, the "you're not my friend" is a device for drawing category lines. Sociologist Junehui Ahn writes, "For children, a friend rarely means someone with whom one makes lasting bonds based on affection, intimacy, and mutual trust, as defined by caregivers. Rather, friends are people whom they can play with and whose social goals converge with their own at certain moments" (2011, 300).

Friends Play Together

For children, friends are people who play together, so "playing together"—initiating play, entering play, defining play, and leaving play—is an incredibly important way that children find and maintain friendships. In his ethnographic research (2011), William Corsaro coins the term "access strategies" and documents the ways in which children attempt to enter play. Children begin by placing themselves in proximity to their peers, attempting to be swept into the flowing river of play. They stand nearby, circling the action as they watch for clues they might use to enter. Soon after, children will often make an entry attempt by bringing a useful object to contribute to the play, or by naturally assuming a role that is missing from the current script. Consider a group of children playing doctor. The uninvolved child might approach carrying a stethoscope as an entry gesture, or will crawl nearby mocking a cry, such as "My leg is broken." Sometimes the ongoing script does not adjust to accommodate the entry attempt, in which case children will make a direct verbal attempt to join by asking, "Can I be a sick baby?" These attempts to enter play carry more significance than just finding something to do; they signify social acceptance and belonging. "Can I be a sick baby?" is a child's way of asking, "Can we be friends?" If the child succeeds in entering play with peers, her place in her social peer network is affirmed. Likewise, failure to enter play carries a deeper significance than simply missing out on fun. Play failures mean breaks in friendship, and those are painful.

These access strategies don't always look like the most effective strategies for entering play. I think of the many times I've watched interactions between adults and children at public parks. Adults stand on the edges of the playground, watching their children *watching other children* play. Adults grow impatient and try to encourage social interaction by saying, "Go ask if she wants to play!" "Look! A friend! Go play with him. I bet he wants to play with you," or "Ooo! She's playing with bubbles. You love bubbles." Without appreciating that this period of observing and circling the play of other children is, in fact, children's attempts to maximize their chances for success, adults believe observant children need help to enter play. What's more, these "helpful suggestions" from adults are often a guaranteed failure for children's entry attempts. Corsaro, who devoted decades to observing children at play, discovered that direct questions such as "Can I play?" were counterproductive to helping children enter play. According to his research, childhood peers interpreted such direct questions as evidence that potential players did not know what was happening, and might cause trouble to the play (2011, 159). As insiders in the culture of childhood, children know they need information from those who are actively playing in order to demonstrate their own value and contribution to an ongoing play script. They know scripts are hard to develop and that new children often unintentionally destroy a script already in progress. Like arriving at a theater halfway through the movie, you must rely on clues from the unfolding scenes to figure out what is going on. Standing up in the theater and asking for help from those who have been there the whole time won't get you very far.

Children's access strategies resemble the strategies adults use when they try to enter conversations with people. Last year I joined a community choir. On the night of my first rehearsal, I felt nervous: what if I couldn't find the correct rehearsal location, or what if people were suspicious of my presence, or what if they didn't think my voice was skilled enough to warrant a place in their group? In short, *what if they didn't want to play with me?* When I arrived, I behaved remarkably like a young child attempting to play with peers. I stayed near the edges of conversations casually listening for a lull so I could make my entry attempt. I cautiously introduced myself, indicating that I was new and asking for practical information about where to sit. The group offered their welcome and brought me into the conversation, helping me find a seat, introducing me to the choir director and the individuals in charge of distributing sheet music. We exchanged names, pleasantries about the day, and basic information about the choir. Basically, I watched from the edges, I found a suitable entry point, and I entered with relevant information. In the end, I was invited to play! Think how different or awkward it would have been for me to walk up to strangers in my new community and say, "Can I talk to you?" "You have to share your music. I'm new and I don't have any yet." Because of social expectations, the adults in my community probably wouldn't have rebuffed my entry attempts, but my presence would have been awkward and uncomfortable.

Sometimes, entry attempts don't look like attempts to play at all. George was four months old when he enrolled in my family child care program, and when he was two, he started pinching and biting his peers. He was a mild-mannered infant and toddler, so this new behavior was troubling and caught me off guard. For days, I tried an assortment of different strategies:

- I was firm, preempting the actual moment of contact by gently blocking George's hands and repeating a reminder: "I won't let you pinch people."

- I redirected the action: "If you need to pinch something, pinch this squishy ball."

- I drew his attention to the impact of his actions: "Ouch! It hurts when you pinch. See her tears? She didn't like that."

- I empowered the victim with words and sign language to thwart the pincers: "Stop! I don't want you to pinch me."

I was stuck; nothing I did was working. I was too focused on the behavior. So one evening, I brainstormed a quick list of possible reasons why George was pinching:

He was curious about what would happen if he pinched.

He was angry with his peers.

He liked the feeling of causing a big reaction.

He wanted to play.

He was already playing.

I spent some time observing and saw that George had developed a game he called "poison meat eaters." This game involved slinking across the play space, teeth bared, imaginary claws flashing, slowly and methodically stalking his "prey." Unfortunately for his peers, *they* were his unwitting prey, and he suddenly pounced on them and pinched or clawed as he satiated his endless appetite. As we will discuss later in this chapter, one of the hallmarks of social connection in the early years is its physicality. When I observed George, what I found was not a mean, naughty child or a bully; instead, I discovered a boy looking for ways to engage socially with his peers—failing, but trying nonetheless. In order to effectively guide his behavior and give him tools to meet his social needs, I had to understand what he was trying to do and support his impulse—not just correct the behavior. He needed supportive access strategies. He needed a model and examples that were culturally responsive.

The next time I saw George baring his claws and moving in for a meal, I, too, sharpened my imaginary claws and joined him in the prowl. We spoke to each other in the gruff, whispery voices of a "poison meat eater." I approached George and initiated a welcome. "Hi." He looked at me, completely unfazed by my new character, as if it were only logical that he might find another poison meat eater to join in the hunt. "Do you see those poisonous animals over there?" I gestured with my head in the direction of the other children. George nodded in affirmation.

"Are we playing with them?" I asked.

George paused for a moment, frozen as the thought penetrated his mind. Without looking back at me, he responded. "Yes."

I continued: "I wonder if they are playing with us. If we claw them, they won't want to play, because it will hurt. Let's watch to see what they are playing." We crouched, partially obscured behind a low bookshelf. The other children were playing a game of king and queen. I narrated in my gruffest, poison-meat-eateriest voice. "It looks like they are playing king and queen. They aren't poisonous animals. Maybe they need a guard for their castle to keep out all the poisonous animals that try to get into the castle. Let's go ask." I was changing his script, so I moved with caution.

"Attention, kings and queens of the castle. We noticed you have a gate here, and there is no one to guard it. What if there is a poisonous animal that tries to enter across the bridge? Can we stay and protect you from any danger?"

The children wholeheartedly agreed. George and I positioned ourselves on the edge of their physical game and occasionally attacked an imaginary incoming animal. Later, we were fed and cared for by the royal court, and put to sleep in the royal stables. I persisted in the play at length on that first day, but as time went on, I was needed less and less. Over meals, the group and I discussed daily events and any problems that arose. I talked to the children about their developing skills, pointing out that George was learning to play with other children, and that his pinching and clawing were actually his way of asking to play. We talked about our own paths to sociability, remembering the mistakes we had all made in entry attempts. Musicians Michael Leeman, Bev Bos, and Tom Hunter sing a powerful song for moments like this, and we relied on their phrase during these mealtime conversations about how much we were learning, growing, and changing: "I remember when you couldn't do that, when you couldn't do that at all" (Leeman, Bos, and Hunter, 2004). We talked about the things we were learning, celebrating moments of growth we observed in each other.

These conversations were reminders that everyone changes, even adults, and we all had a role to play in each other's learning.

Recognizing George's clawing and pinching as signs of social connection, or the behavior of children on the edges of play as signs of social competency, or the pounding of toddlers around a shared table as an act of creating friendship requires a shift in thinking. It requires understanding that children see friendships differently than adults, that children learn to access and maintain friendships differently than adults might imagine, and that children are competent social actors in the development of their social worlds.

Exclusionary Play in the Culture of Childhood

What about times when childhood behaviors appear to dismantle social ties? Whole sections of early years curriculum are devoted to teaching children what it means to be a friend, but those definitions are often at odds with the actual daily happenings in early childhood environments. Educators teach that friends share. Friends comfort one another. Friends let other friends play. Friends are kind. Friends speak using gentle words. Friends use gentle hands. But our field has fallen into a trap of expecting children to realize some kind of nonreality in which everyone will be friends with everyone, no one will be left out, and everyone will always be polite. On the surface this sounds like a good ideal to strive toward. Personal experiences with the pain of exclusion and acts of cruelty, along with research about the devastating impacts of bullying on both victim and aggressor, add an element of urgency to this work.

But there's a catch. Actual friendship is never this idealized fantasy. Friendship is complex, and healthy friendships are built on an element of exclusion. As an adult, I have the power to choose friends who bring me joy and enrich my life. I can choose to exclude those who are demanding, hurtful, or demeaning. I can be selective among my friends with the information that I share; not every friend knows all the intimate parts of my life. I don't have to be friends with everyone. As early childhood educators, our responsibility is to make sure children have the *chance* to be friends with everyone, not the *duty* to be friends with everyone. Our responsibility to young children is to support their development of authentic relationships instead of blanketing every social interaction in a kind of idealized fantasy in which every human being is always *nice* to everyone else.

Children have the right to be angry when their play is ruined or interrupted by another child. If I work hard to build a tower and someone knocks it down, I am rightfully angry. If that same person knocks over my tower a second and a third time, I am rightfully wary of including her in the future. I can ask for help from my teachers without worrying that those teachers are going to patronize my request for protected work space with a simple, "I'm sure she didn't mean it," or "I bet we can find a game that *everyone* wants to play."

Let's look closely at a scenario involving a group of three- and four-year-old boys playing together in a corner of Meg's classroom. They have fashioned a six-inch-high fence made of unit blocks lined up end to end, reaching from one wall to another, symbolically cutting off the corner of a square classroom, creating a wedge of boys isolated in spirit from the rest of the group. With the fence in position, they turn their attention inward, moving to phase two of construction. Jean, an eager and boisterous three-year-old girl, wanders over to where the boys are playing, unaware of the low block fence or its purpose in demarcating this group of boys from everyone else. Stepping right over it, she moves her way into the thick flurry of activity.

"No fair!" yells Max.

"Get out!" hollers Romain. "We're playing here."

"No girls allowed!" chides Lucas.

Jean is surprised by the unanticipated verbal assault from this gaggle of her playing peers. Moving quickly from surprise to insult, she begins to cry and grabs the first object she sees—a wooden unit block formerly known to the boys as "fence"—and hits Lucas over the head until he also starts to cry. Meg, noting the rising commotion, moves from walk to run in order to intervene on behalf of the screaming children. She arrives in a few seconds and neutralizes the swinging block. Gathering the red-faced Jean and Lucas on her lap, she wades full force into the minefield known as "What happened here?"

She assembles fragments of heavy sobs into a story, summarized as follows:

The boys were working on a project.

Jean knocked over their fence.

The boys told Jean that girls were not allowed to play with them.

Jean hit Lucas on the head with a block from the fence.

Facts in hand, Meg walks the children through a reconstruction effort made up of "Blocks are not for hitting and we are all friends here" to "Can we come up with a game that includes everyone?" The boys, who formerly played with the buzz of scientists on the verge of a discovery, now appear as slack-sailed sailboats that have lost the wind, floating at sea and moving listlessly with the rolling waves. The coed group feigns an attempt at collaborative construction before Max suggests a game of hide-and-seek and the group abandons the blocks altogether, leaving a partially constructed fence of unit blocks standing like the remains of the Roman Colosseum, reminiscent of purposeful play.

In their attempt to create shared interactive space—one of the cornerstones of authentic friendship—children work hard to protect their friendships from potential threats. The first threat to friendship is interruptions. Interruptions are highly disorienting, and the time it takes to recover from an interruption can interfere with the depth of exploration. Children are acutely aware of their powerlessness in the face of these interruptions, contending with such play interrupters as cleanup or lunchtime. They know that at any time their toys might be taken away and redistributed to someone else who has been waiting for a turn, so when nonplayers try to join a game, the children who were already playing will reject them to protect against interruption. Educators Elizabeth Jones and Renatta Cooper share a revealing conversation

Jones overheard between her two children. An older brother was giving his younger sister some advice about kindergarten: "No point in starting anything there. They never let you finish. Don't get interested. You'll just get interrupted" (2006, 23). Because children live with the reality that their play attempts might be interrupted at any moment, they defend their play fiercely. Any interruption—peer, teacher, the daily schedule—is seen as an enemy of friendship.

A second threat to friendship is the adult goal of blanket inclusivity, or forced friendship. When Meg forces Jean into the play, the script dissolves and the boys change games. For children to build meaningful friendships in the early years, they need help protecting the interactive space that is critical to maintaining a play rhythm. "Friendship," says Corsaro, "means producing shared activity together in a specific area and protecting that play from the intrusions of others" (2011, 161). Sometimes, what appears "mean" is actually just children trying to protect their deep play. Unfortunately, educators often arrive on the scene alongside Meg, and we don't see what happened before the first block was thrown. We don't see the boys' intense desire to play, or their competency in trying to prevent Jean from playing. We interpret their comments as mean, even charged with bias because of the comments directed toward Jean because she's a girl, when their desires come from an intense drive to play together. They are trying to create a shared experience; they are trying to be friends. Jean represents a threat to those goals.

Forced friendship is more than not friendship; it undermines the bonds that could be friendship and cauterizes them. Forced friendships are like anti-friendships, removing children from the whole process, usurping their ability to be empathetic and reach out to connect with each other. When we force children to include one another, we unwittingly teach them three things. First, listening to their inner voice about people is not as important as being nice or *friendly* to everyone. In *It's OK Not to Share and Other Renegade Rules for Raising Competent and Compassionate Kids*, Heather Shumaker makes the bold claim that "we're not *all* friends" to counter the ubiquitous mantra of early childhood settings (2012). Second, we destroy the child's sense of control. Ironically, if we empower children to be decision makers in their play, they are far more generous with their time and their resources than if we interfere. If we continuously take charge of their play, then they will have no choice but to use power to control each other. Third, we burden children's social development with a kind of protective bubble wrap that prevents them from developing the lifelong skills necessary to face social challenges with confidence. Children who develop resilience in the face of social rejection will rebound when they are fired from a job or rejected by a romantic partner. Rejection will always be painful, but through experience, they learn what we need to recover from that pain. What a powerful testament to the importance of childhood interactions, that adults would choose to support authentic social skills rather than fake friendship!

The act of social exclusion is often evidence of social capacity rather than social lack. Children are trying to continue sharing, and they perceive the intrusion of a new player as disastrous. The solution is not forced friendship or a generic "we're all friends here!" Because children understand friends to be the people they are interacting with in the moment, the threat of exclusion is a real fear for them. We have work to do with peers on both sides of the exclusionary line. On the one hand, children who are actively excluding others need our help to do so with sensitivity and tact. On the other hand, the peers who are rejected need reassurance that the friendship can resume once the play is ended, and they need help learning to wait.

Let's return to the example of the three boys who were building a fence before Jean came along to play. This time, when Meg arrives at the scene and neutralizes the block Jean is swinging, she proceeds differently. The boys tell their side of the story and Jean offers her own. Amends are made for the block injury, and the children begin to process the event with Meg.

MEG: "So it sounds to me like you three were playing and Jean interrupted."

LUCAS: "Yes! She knocked over our fence!"

MEG: "I bet Jean was very curious about what you were doing."

JEAN: "I want to play, too!"

MEG: "I see. You want to play. It sounds like the boys are playing right now. I wonder if there is a spot for you to play, too?"

ROMAIN: "No. She can't play with us now."

MEG: "Then you can tell Jean, 'We are playing now, but maybe we can play together another time.' "

ROMAIN: "Jean, we're playing now, but maybe we can play together another time."

MEG: [to Jean] "I will help you wait. What should we do while we wait?"

The boys continue with their construction.

Creating a Socially Supportive Environment

Children understand friendship in a different way than adults, and when we begin to see their social connections through the cultural lens of childhood, we begin to recognize their great social competencies rather than their social deficits. Even behaviors that seem antisocial can be deeply social, as children strive to protect the interactive space necessary for meaningful social connections with one another. As early childhood professionals, we can take steps to help ensure that our environments and our practice support the sophisticated social structure of childhood. In creating programs designed with the culture of childhood in mind, we are creating "culturally aware" programs.

Culturally Aware Programs Are Highly Physical Places

Young children create shared experiences with their bodies through actions such as running, dancing, jumping, falling, pushing, pulling, kicking, and climbing. Babies and toddlers, in particular, communicate with their social community through their bodies. Young babies make eye contact and kick their feet against the ground when eye contact is returned. They learn to point and follow the gestures of loved ones. Toddlers say "Good morning" by jumping up and down and hugging their friends and they say "I'm sorry" by offering their special stuffed animals in empathy or as an apology. They affirm their friendship through loud, repetitive games that anyone can enter.

Toddlers Christopher (twenty-eight months) and Jonah (thirty months) have just arrived for the day. They run together around the classroom laughing and screaming, and when they reach a pile of cushions, they take turns falling in dramatic fashion. Loud sounds of *woah!* echo in the room as the boys fall over and over again. Typically, we respond to children like Christopher and Jonah by quieting them and directing them to walk not run. But what if, instead, we recognize that these two boys are welcoming one another? That by the nature of their toddlerhood, such welcomes take the form of running and yelling and participating in this shared act of joy as they fall over and over?

Would this adjusted perception change the way we respond to their activity? Perhaps there are important safety reasons to restrict their running or falling, but perhaps there are ways to support their moment of connection by recognizing it and valuing it for what it is. Perhaps we could look for ways to make our programs safe for running by leaving wide walkways or demarcating paths with masking tape on the floor. We could teach children to watch out for their peers while they run so they don't knock into each other. We could designate which spaces are protected running spaces and which ones are not.

The social structure of young children is intensely physical. Children are physical with their positive feelings toward one another and also physical with their anger and frustration. Not every child, however, wants to be hugged by an energetic peer when they first arrive; in fact, many children like time to warm up before running around the room and screaming. We can help children channel their energies in ways that support the physical needs of the entire community:

Talk about how it feels to be excited to see someone. Help children find ways to wait for their friends to share their excitement. Offer the opportunity to run up and say hello to new arrivals while keeping a small distance. Give nonverbal clues to all the children so that when they arrive, they can show a sign to their peers that communicates, "I need some space."

If we know children engage in their social community through physical interactions, we can make space for those to happen, even indoors. Clear a continuous path around the furniture so that when children want to run, there is a safe place to do it. Add elements like giant pillows for climbing or mattresses for jumping.

Teach children nonverbal ways to communicate their strong emotions. We often ask children to "use their words" when they are angry, but it would be far more effective if we also gave them a physical action for demonstrating their anger. Clapping their hands together hard, stomping their feet, gritting their teeth and growling, and waving their hands are all examples of physical motions that can communicate deep feelings of anger, frustration, or disappointment. Children need physical ways to communicate all sorts of feelings to their social network.

Give physical signals for phrases such as, "I'm not done yet." and "Can I have it?" Again, if children have something physical to do, they don't need to hit or bite or kick each other. Even as children do develop verbal language, for a long time that verbal language may not be as natural for them as using their physical bodies. I am learning French, but it will be a long time before I naturally use French to communicate my deep feelings.

Culturally Aware Programs Are Full of Big, Heavy, Full-Body Materials

Adults are biased to believe that the early years are angst- and conflict-ridden, but, notes Gunvor Løkken (2000), this perception may be based on our lack of understanding of the young child's culture. In her detailed review of research into toddler relationships, Løkken observes a cooperative, empathetic, and communal culture. When toddlers are allowed to use their whole bodies in concert with their peers, they no longer have a need for conflict. Løkken hypothesizes that a lot of toddler conflict has to do with materials. Small materials are typically designed to be manipulated by children working individually, or by groups of children working collectively, but still independently. Think about children building with train tracks. Only one child can work with each piece at a time, and even if there are multiple children building with multiple pieces of track, that action has to be coordinated in order to arrive at a product that works. For toddlers, who have such an overwhelming need to engage bodily with their peer community, these materials sometimes create a situation in which children end up hitting, kicking, throwing, and taking toys. Even though these are undesirable behaviors, their roots are a drive for social connection.

Løkken observes the ways in which large materials invite group participation. Toddlers can work together to accomplish a collective goal using objects such as tree stumps that can be moved from one side of the yard to another, a deep sandbox where toddlers can dig a giant hole together, jumping mats where toddlers can tumble together, laundry baskets that can be filled and pushed, large water pails that children can fill and dump, and big cardboard boxes or blocks that children can pile, stack, and carry. When many children are able to use the same materials together in a collective experience, there is much less confrontation.

Culturally Aware Programs Allow Children to Say No

When we see that a child's "no" can be a sign of social competency, we can look for ways to support it. We can help children learn to draw social lines in compassionate ways. Children use language in different ways than we do, so when boys say, "No girls allowed!" they aren't necessarily lobbing a sexist comment; they are simply trying to protect an ongoing interactive space and using a broad social category to draw boundaries. Programs can establish guidelines such as "You don't have to be friends, but you have to be kind." We can help students learn to say no with respect to the person they are rejecting.

Give children compassionate and respectful language to protect play:

> "We're playing now, but you can play with us later."

> "After I'm done with this game, you and I can play a game together."

Give children language to include a new peer:

> "You can't be a dinosaur, because we don't need a dinosaur. But you can be an elephant. Do you want to be an elephant?"

Give children planning language and writing support that can help them create lists and verbalize desires to help during the waiting time:

> "I am playing trucks now, but I want to play kings and queens later. Do you want to play later? Let's write down our plan."

Culturally Aware Programs Minimize Interruptions

When children know their right to play without being interrupted will be protected, they are free to include others. When they know they will have the time they need to finish a project, they are free to invest the time into incorporating another player. Even with these provisions in place, children may still draw protective barriers around their play. But they have the greatest chance and are the most open to considering peers if they know they won't be interrupted and will have time.

Have you ever noticed how lengthy the process of preparing to play can be? All of the conversation about who will play what character and how the props will be distributed—it takes a long time. Spaces built around lots of interruption prevent children from being able to play to their full extent. There are enough natural interruptions without us adding more. In our programs, let's rethink our use of centers and short, truncated blocks of time that keep children in perpetual transition.

Practitioners in Culturally Aware Early Childhood Spaces Have Room for Observation

Building time to sit and observe children interacting with one another is one of the most powerful ways to affirm children's competency. If we are too busy in the background, we—like Meg in the earlier story—miss those opportunities. When we sit to observe, we see toddlers offering their special trinkets to peers who are sad when their parents leave. We see children creatively incorporating less-skilled players into their script, mentoring their movement with the group. We see babies making eye contact with the other children in the program and smiling. We notice how laughter draws all children together as a symbol of community, and we are drawn to laugh with them. Think twice before setting up a highly involved activity and, instead, choose to sit close to the children in your care and watch for moments of competency. The more you look, the more you will see, and the more it will confirm your practice.

Stories from the Field

TRAPS AND MAPS

by Lakisha Reid

Our deep exploration of traps and maps started simply with the ever so popular girls vs. boys schema we see so often in early childhood and beyond. As educators we observed this play, looking for its deeper meaning, its purpose, what the children were getting or not getting out of it. As we focused on observation and understanding, as opposed to just shutting down the experience, we began to notice that this play had rich purpose.

At its root, this play served as a way for the children to find belonging. Strange, right? Finding belonging by excluding? As we observed, we learned to see the play as more of a sorting into groups based on commonality, connecting and finding a sense of belonging. The most obvious category for the children was commonality based on gender, so that was the criterion they used.

At times, exclusion filled the play; it got uncomfortable in some cases, but that only seemed to fuel the deep play that was going on. The discomfort belonged to the adults; the children seemed to be immersed in play. As I reflect on the play I remember children feeling powerful, full of joy, vigor, excitement, and experiencing full body play. Surprisingly, there was no real exclusion happening. Everyone was allowed to play. Two teams were totally enthralled in one play experience. It was not until the day the children were all dressed in armor, gowns, and crowns, and armed with paper towel tube swords, that one very quiet girl came out of her shell. She protected her turf, twirling and shouting, "Hi-yah!" She was *powerful* both physically and emotionally. This game had come alive for them all.

This rich play, with story lines full of great detail, developed over time. Teachers spent much time transcribing the dictated stories of castles, dragons, and dungeons. We all shared them together and many times the reading of these stories sparked new and exciting play. One constant element was the making of traps. Water tables became elaborate "traps to catch the girls," while webs of tape around the classroom transformed into boy-catching traps.

Although on the surface the children seemed to be dividing the community, a deeper look revealed the closeness they were developing; the feeling of power experienced by both the boys and the girls served as the glue that kept them coming back for more.

Over time we began to notice that the lines between boys and girls blurred. The original guideline they used to sort themselves evolved. Children who enjoyed building traps began to work together on projects regardless of sex; children who enjoyed the planning phase gathered to draw large detailed maps and plans for the trap makers; and the scriptwriters dictated detailed scenes. This collaboration promoted an authentic child-led project that spanned an entire school year. The educators supported this passion by adding and replenishing an abundant supply of open-ended materials to be used to assemble traps: large rolls and sheets of paper, rulers, atlases, books, and resources full of photographs of real castles. The most important thing we gave the children was trust in play and time and space to explore it deeply.

Lakisha Reid is owner and educator at Discovery Early Learning Center and founder of Play Empowers, an advocacy community of reflective learners who support each other as they seek to elevate the quality of early childhood programs and the early childhood field as a whole. Lakisha has worked directly with children and families for over twenty years in a variety of settings from large centers and summer camps to small home-based programs and kindergarten classrooms.

Stories from the Field

NO FORCED APOLOGIES

by Melissa Cady

It was one of those dry, hot afternoons in California. The kind where the dirt turns to dust and paints the sweaty arms, necks, and legs of little children. All of the children were exhausted after a long day in a full-day care program yet still happily and loudly playing in the yard. I was one of three teachers supervising the large group as they played while waiting to be picked up. The youngest in the group and in only my second year of teaching, I was often second-guessing my theories and philosophy among a group who had been teaching since I was in middle school.

Two of the children kept catching my eye. A three-year-old girl and a boy who was slightly older by several months. They were laughing hysterically and playing a game that was getting more and more physical. My perception was that they were on the edge. Chasing each other and falling to the ground, running circles around one another, gently wrestling and then getting up to start all over again. They were pushing the boundaries of exhaustion, emotions, social relations, and all that entails for children that age. They were full of the excitement of connection and friendship, but I felt they would be unable to handle it if something upset the balance.

The little girl's mom walked through our sliding door to the yard and I braced myself. The duo ran away, stating they wouldn't go, wouldn't be separated. The mother followed and persisted. She got down on her daughter's level, gently touched her shoulder, and said, "It's time to go, we are leaving now. Would you like to say bye?" Reluctantly, the girl sighed, rested on her mother's leg, and said, "Okay, byeeee," in a singsong voice. The boy's face fell. His fun was leaving. He looked so devastated.

In an effort to keep the fun going, he started making funny jokes, using classic three-year-old humor. They were still leaving. He grabbed the little girl's leg. I had been close but came closer now. "She is leaving, how can I help you? Would you like to come with me?" He reached down into the dry dirt, which was full of leaves and tan bark, picked up a fistful, and threw it in the little girl's face. Instantly it filled her eyes. She screamed, cried, and yelled for her mom.

I could feel the eyes of the other two teachers on me. I could hear their narrative in my head. "Say you're sorry!" "What were you thinking?" "Why did you do that?" I could feel the pressure to raise my voice and firmly put him in time-out.

Instead, I got close, held his hands, and watched his face. He hid his eyes from me. "That really surprised her, her eyes are full of dirt. What can we do?" He ran behind me and crouched down. Again the lump in my throat and my burning ears were telling me that I was being judged, but I just couldn't shame him any more. He was obviously full of shame already. I wanted to be his support. I wanted to give him a chance for closure without making him feel worse. "She is going to leave soon. Is there any-thing we should do?" "I don't have to say sorry!" he yelled at me. "No, you don't," I replied, "but maybe we should see if she's okay? Shall we check together?" He reached out his hand and we walked over to her. He quietly asked his friend if she was okay; she shyly answered back and started to leave with her mom. He turned his back and started to walk away. Then suddenly he turned around, hands on his hips and with a strong voice called out, "I'm so sorry! I didn't know it would fly at you like that!" With that I think both he and I let out a sigh of relief and we walked back to the yard.

Melissa Cady is an early childhood educator and the owner of The Garden, a family child care program located in the East Bay of California. She holds a bachelor's of arts in community studies from the University of California at Santa Cruz. For the past ten years she has formally and informally studied early childhood education while working as an educator, administrator, and mentor. Melissa has owned her own family child care program for two years and enjoys the freedom she has to work within her deeply rooted philosophical beliefs.

CHAPTER THREE

"We're Stuck!"
The Language of Childhood

"People who live together need to create a culture together, in order to make connections with one another and assure themselves that their time together is of value."

—Elizabeth Jones
and Gretchen Reynolds

A FEW YEARS AGO, I WAS WORKING with a cohort of people to plan an event. During one of our meetings, the director of the group asked for ideas, and I spoke up. One of the other women in the group attacked me, dismissing my ideas as thoughtless and irresponsible. Clearly, what I'd said had touched a nerve with this person. I felt my face flush and my heartbeat quicken. I was hurt by the undeserved attack. Seated in the group, I bit the inside of my cheek to keep from crying.

I kept it together until I reached my car, where I promptly burst into tears. I sobbed in a full-body kind of way, grateful that it was dark outside so my sorrow was hidden from nearby drivers. I immediately sent a text message to my partner; I was too emotional to talk. For the entire drive home, I talked myself through the exchange, saying out loud in the safety of my car what I would have liked to say in the meeting. When I got home, I told my partner the whole story. Then I called a friend, and then my mom. The more I told the story, the more I was able to make sense of the experience. This woman was not attacking me, she was lashing out because of a larger backstory that had little to do with me. My anger was justified, but contextualizing her comments was a relief. Through the conversations I had with my loved ones, I was able to make meaning out of this hurtful experience and find healing.

Language Makes Meaning

The next cultural category we will explore is language. A cultural system of language is complex, formed in part by vocabulary, grammar, and syntax, and defined by both verbal and nonverbal elements. Language is the communication tool of a culture as well as a mechanism for processing and making meaning. After that terrible meeting, I had to externalize the events I experienced out loud to myself and with my closest friends and family. Language is a tool used by many for communicating and for processing.

Typically, when we think about children and language, we think about language acquisition, and how and when children gain verbal communication skills; we may quickly assume the language of childhood is composed of our work in preliteracy. Babies babble and coo in order to wire their neural pathways for language. Toddlers use broad language categories such as "dog" when referencing any animal, as they begin to experiment with the function of language. Four- and five-year-olds grow more sophisticated in their language use, generalizing grammar rules, for example, adding an *s* to the end of a word to make it plural. The problem, though, is that a system of language is so much more than appropriate use of vocabulary (word choice) and grammar (the principles and rules concerning word order and syntax).

Young children are still developing spoken language, and yet their ability to make meaning of the world is robust. Author and educator Ruth Forbes points out that the origins of the word *infant* reveal a residual bias about a child's ability to communicate: "'Infant' comes from the Latin 'infans,' meaning 'unable to speak.' To call our babies 'infants' does not do them justice—we know that although they might not yet have the words, they certainly are able to communicate" (2004, 109). To accurately describe the language system of childhood, we need to broaden our definition of language. Consider the following story, and the ways in which the children involved processed and made meaning out of the situation.

Bordering the backyard of my family child care program was an empty field with piles of dirt, and it was in this field that I had one of my most memorable days as a child care provider. An unseasonable February thaw had melted most of the snow, leaving the ground saturated with water. The children and I donned our boots and spent the morning playing at a local neighborhood park. After a full morning of gathering sticks for makeshift huts, foraging in the mud for treasures, climbing on the slide, and stomping in the puddles, we headed for home, passing this empty lot and the enticing dirt that was now mud.

The children began to implore, "Emily! Can we go stomp in the mud?" I was thinking of the tasks I had ahead of me: prepare lunch, help the children change from a day of wet and muddy play at the park, begin the transition toward naptime, but I was persuaded by the abundant joy that is locked away inside natural elements like mud. Besides, since they were already to an extent wet and muddy from the park, it seemed like a reasonable pursuit. "Go ahead. But we can't stay too long because we need to go home and get ready for lunch."

One by one, the children raced ahead. The first child broke off the path and took her first steps into the giant puddle. She immediately stopped short. "Emily! I'm *stuck*!" Her feet were firmly vacuumed to the ground in an inch of soft, wet mud. Before I could reach her, the next child in the long line of children running toward the field shouted, "Don't worry—I'll help you!" and in she went to the mud puddle, where she promptly also became stuck.

From my place at the rear of the line, I yelled to the children, "No one else go in the mud! I'm coming!" but my voice fell empty alongside the string of children who were bent on helping each other out of the mud. One by one, they ran to save their peers, and one by one, they all got stuck in the mud. This whole scene unfolded in a matter of a few moments, but it was happening for me in slow motion. I was pushing a stroller with our youngest strapped inside (at least one child would not get stuck in the mud). By the time I came to the edge of the mud puddle, six children were locked in place. Two were crying hysterically, one had stepped out of her boot by accident and her foot was stuck in the deep mud, and several were pondering the *what if*s that might accompany such a predicament. My own mind was racing—I had no protocol for a mud rescue! So I did what any normal, levelheaded adult would do. I went in the mud after them.

Can you guess what happened? Seven people got stuck! My mind raced from panic (What do I do now?) to concern (What will my clients think of me for *this* one?) to fleeting amusement (Ha! We are quite a bunch!) to logistical problems (What is the procedure for 'Children Stuck In Mud'—do I call 911? Will they send a hook and ladder truck to rescue us?) to outwardly reassuring the children (We'll get out of here. We can solve all of our problems!). In addition to the spectacle of seven human beings stuck in the mud, several of whom were hysterical, passersby on the nearby path had stopped to stare. No one on the path said anything, they just watched like bystanders at a terrible accident scene. I feel immense pressure when I am out in public with my grand bunch, so this gawking audience was not helping. Imagine the scene— six stuck children, one stuck adult, and a baby in a stroller.

I finally discovered that I could move my own feet if I grabbed my heavy snow boots by the laces and pulled hard. In this way, I managed to make my way to one of the children. I grabbed her by the arms and tried to lift her out of the mud. I pulled and pulled, but she would not come lose. Eventually, I decided to unfasten her boots, and pull her straight out of her shoes, free from the mud. When she was in my arms, I lobbed her to the safety of the mud-free ground nearby. Without the weight of a child, I was able to wiggle her boots free and toss them out after her. It took about ten minutes before I had successfully dislodged everyone from the mud. At that point, we were all a little shaken up by the experience. The children's mud-streaked faces emitted palpable relief, and they chatted with each other with residual nervous energy. Everyone had stopped crying, and we all marched, mud-caked, back to the house.

That day, as we sat around cheesy noodles and green beans, we processed the day in grand retellings of our moments stuck in the mud. We wrote and illustrated a story about the day we got stuck in the mud, and in the days and weeks that followed, the children played games called "We're Stuck!" with themes of danger and rescue. There were cries for help from various corners of the room, calm reassuring words from the adult characters in the plays, and lots of talk about mud. The way the children made meaning out of this experience gives us a clue into the child's culture of language.

Play as Language

Throughout the early years, children's first and most powerful language in communicating and meaning making is play. Theirs is a *performative* language, built through the bodily and verbal interactions they have with one another as well as with adults. It is through play that babies define their visual field, converse with loved ones, and discover object permanence. Through play, toddlers perfect their mobility, find the limits of their behavior, and cultivate the early seeds of empathic connection to others. Through play, children grapple with power and fairness, develop the strength to persist and negotiate, and understand the mysterious worlds they inhabit. Play is the means by which children make sense of their world, bringing all life events into the safety of their imaginations.

Through the act of playing, children assimilate all their life experiences from the memorable to the mundane, reviewing the moments step by step in order to develop a deep understanding of the way the world works. Consider the scripts children incorporate into their daily play lives. In the days following a field trip to the library on public transportation, the children in my child care program played bus. In the days following an intense series of tornado drills and power outages, they played emergency drill. When a family in our program had a new baby born by Cesarean, I heard conversations between the children in my care about how they were "going to go have a C-section now. Be back soon!" The same children would later pretend to nurse their new-born babies. In the absence of anything out of the ordinary, children are hard at work processing the daily life of human beings they admire with themes such as work, school, babies, grocery store, hotel, camping, and firefighters. In their conversations, we hear echoes of their experiences as they reverse the power roles. They decide who gets a shot at a visit to the doctor, and they become the doctor capable of wielding that painful but powerful elixir. They decide when it is time for the babies to sleep, and they become the parents who demand that their squirrelly children lie down and close their eyes. They decide when the magic powers work to bring life, and they mix the potions and wave the wands that are capable of anything. In play, children find a variety of voices they do not have in their families and child care settings.

In early childhood programs, play is not just "a good idea." Play is not something children do to pass time, and it isn't what adults "allow" children to do when the day's lesson plans have run out. True, authentic play is not organized and scripted by adults; it is as essential to a growing human body as eating, sleeping, or breathing. The drive to play is fierce but over time it will fade, dampened by the pervasive and passive entertainment of digital media, the sedentary monotony of structured schooling and activities, and the constant messages about its insignificance and worthlessness.

The culture of adulthood faces significant challenges when it comes to understanding play. We don't really get what children are doing; we lack a metaphor that recognizes the significance of their endeavor. Our linguistic pendulum swings between the extremes of play as work and play as fun, but both miss the mark. We work hard to defend the *learning* that takes place as a way of justifying time spent playing. We struggle with stakeholders who believe children need more structure and shouldn't spend the whole day "just playing." Even though we grew up playing and used play to successfully make our transition from birth to adulthood, we have assimilated too completely into the culture of adulthood and lost fluency with our first language. As children, we played because it was fun. We played because it nurtured relationships with the people around us. We played because we were absolutely com-pelled, from the core of our beings, to do so.

When I study play, I continue to come back to a basic question. Why is play suspect? Why don't we trust it? If there is one area of childhood that does not suffer for lack of research, it's the importance of play. My shelves are overflowing with books documenting its value, purpose, shape, and necessity. We have study after study that traces the roots of adult maladjustment and antisocial behavior to a play-deprived childhood (Brown 2010). With the abundance of research to prove that play is perhaps the single best way for children to create a meaningful foundation for their adult lives, *why don't we believe it?*

Stuart Brown, founder of the National Institute for Play, describes the opposition between true adulthood and play: "The message is that if you are a serious person doing serious work, you should be serious. Seriously" (2010, 145). He explains that we operate with a "culturally supported idea that people who play are superficial, are not living in the real world, are dilettantes or amoral slackers" (147). We take pride in our hard work and brag to others about how little free time we have. We wear our full schedules like badges of honor, the chimes and chirps of our electronic devices announcing to the world how important and busy we are. We collect accolades from others in our community who cannot understand *how* we do it all. We have acquiesced to the notion that play belongs in the domain of childhood, placing it at odds with the serious pursuits of adulthood.

Play is considered, at best, an accessory to *real* learning, and by the time children enter kindergarten, they are expected to learn in *real* ways: sitting in chairs, raising their hands, quietly working on worksheets. Consequently, the task of early childhood educators has become "kindergarten readiness." Children should have competency with certain academic skills such as knowing the alphabet, numbers, days of the week, and how to write their names. They should control their bathroom needs, know how to ask an adult for help, listen to a story without interrupting, pay attention to adult-directed tasks, and sit without becoming distracted for a discussion of the day's agenda and calendar items. I have yet to read a list of kindergarten readiness skills that includes the true, culturally relevant pursuits of early childhood, for example, initiating play with peers, advocating for the needs of self and others in the midst of peer conflicts, and accommodating shifts in a play script. In part, our quest for kindergarten readiness is evidence of our futuristic bias toward childhood, and leaning in to play is an alternative to the mind-set that keeps us firmly rooted in the present.

The purpose of this chapter is not to make the case for play; lots of books already do that quite well and I've included some useful titles in the resources section. Instead, I want to explore the cultural function of play as language. From a place of understanding, we will resist our urge to interrupt, script, overrule, manipulate, and dictate the play of young children. The focus of this chapter is to situate play as a language and to think of it as a strategy for communicating and meaning making.

Remembering a Forgotten Language

We can examine play from every angle imaginable, and in so doing we will find thousands of reasons to support its value. And still, the broader culture of adulthood has mistaken maturity for seriousness and situated "real life" in opposition to playfulness. Reconnecting with the emotion of play is one of the surest ways to find our way back to this forgotten language. No amount of hard evidence or analysis will help us regain our fluency with the language of play. Stuart Brown offers a helpful simile about play: "If we leave the emotion of play out of the science, it's like throwing a dinner party and serving pictures of food" (2010, 20–21).

Understanding the behind-the-scenes work that children do when they play is important, particularly if we hope to design programs that honor this child-led pursuit. If we are to defend it, we must believe that what children are doing is important. But to truly see for ourselves the deep significance of play, we need to experience the emotion of it, and capture the authenticity and joy of our children at play. We need to squish our boots into mud without worrying about cleaning up, lie on the floor to watch rainbows on the ceiling, skip to the grocery store, make hair out of playdough pushed through a garlic press, swing on the swings at the park, scream as loudly as we can, run as fast as we can, jump as high as we can, read a book for fun, build a fort and play with flashlights, eat ice cream for breakfast, or fly a kite. Tapping into the emotion of play compels us to defend our children's right to play because we are reminded of its transformative impact. In experiencing the emotion of play, we develop a kind of bicultural fluency, the ability to connect both with adults in the language of adulthood and with children in the language of childhood.

My partner's ancestors are from Serbia; his grandfather immigrated to the United States when he was three. In an effort to fit in, the family stopped speaking Serbian at home and required the children to speak English. After three generations in the United States, few Serbian words remain. The few that do seem to be either relational, such as *Baba* and *Jedo* (Grandmother and Grandfather), or mildly inappropriate, like *guzitsa* (butt/ass).

If we do retain any connections to our language of play as adults, they seem to fit a similar pattern—they are relational (poker games with colleagues or games of basketball on the weekends) or they are mildly inappropriate (pranks at work or posting cat memes on Facebook). The play of adults is usually highly organized and structured when compared with our younger playing counterparts. Adults tend to engage in premeditated play events. "Would you like to come over to play poker this Friday night?" Our play lacks the spontaneity of young children. Once all your friends arrive at your house for a game of poker, you would rarely deviate from the plan and instead, say, build paper airplanes or have a bubble-gum-blowing contest.

To truly engage with children in their language of play, we must ourselves begin to play in ways that reflect the patterns of children. We must practice playing in the context of our adult lives, not just engaging in play with the children in our care during working hours. We must flex our playful muscles by engaging in impromptu pickup basketball games or joining an improv comedy team. To engage in real and authentic play, our pursuits should be spontaneous, be voluntary, lack a defined goal, contain an element of make-believe, and require our active engagement (Hirsh-Pasek and Golinkoff 2003, 210–11). To be honest, this is a difficult proposition for most adults, including me. I am not, by nature, particularly playful. The nature of play, to me, often feels frivolous and uncomfortable. At the same time, in those moments when I experience true play, I find my senses awakened in new and rejuvenating ways.

In spring 2014, our family sailed around the world with a college program called Semester at Sea. This program allows students from across the United States and around the world to apply to join a shipboard community along with faculty and other staff to spend a semester of their college experience taking classes on the ship and traveling to countries around the world. My partner was a staff member on board, and my children and I accompanied as a part of a cohort of family members along for the experience.

Toward the end of the voyage, the students held a "headphones dance party." Everyone was invited. The premise was that you downloaded a premade audio playlist to an mp3 player, and, donning headphones, joined the group in one of the main student centers on the ship. The mp3 track was a thirty-minute mixed tape of sorts, combining familiar songs across a wide range of genres, interspersed with instructions. At one point, we were instructed to divide into two groups and toss a shoe into the middle of the room to find a waltz partner. At another point, we were instructed to make whale noises and pretend to swim. What made this experience particularly funny was that we were all listening to the same thing, but observers who were not participating had no idea what we were hearing. Nonparticipants gathered to watch our oddly synchronized group parade through the ship. The final songs ended on one of the top decks. Staring out at the vast, black night ocean, I was moved to tears by a sense of connection to the others with whom I had shared this play experience, as well as deeply moved by this absurd act of sanctioned silliness. I kept the audio file and occasionally I cue it up on my phone, reentering the fun of that night.

I observed something else that evening. I watched as this group of college students took a break from their intense studying to play. Finals were approaching, and the stress on the ship was palpable. As we danced, I sensed the release. Adults are disconnected from the ability to play that we once had as children, and yet the need to play remains like the phantom pains from an amputated limb. We have excised play from our lives, but the need for it remains. Some large companies are recognizing the importance of play and are soliciting the expertise of folks like Stuart Brown of the National Institute for Play to help them invite more play into the workplace, understanding that time at play is not a distraction from important work but rather the means to important work.

How can we find our way back to this forgotten language of play? In part, we must revisit a time when our own primary language was play. As a child, did you love reptiles? Did you construct elaborate small-scale buildings? Did you draw and cut out and glue things? Did you paint? Did you take apart toasters and old machines? Did you design rockets? Tapping into some of the activities in which we found joy as children can be the first step to remembering how to play. One way to start to remember how to play is to consider the pieces of your childhood that you pursued at the expense of everything else, the activity that you had to be pried from in order to eat or sleep.

When I find myself lacking inspiration as a parent and an educator, fumbling to write my way through another chapter, or emotionally lost in a difficult situation with a friend, I reorient myself in spontaneous ways that connect with my passions—like spinning down the hall instead of walking in a straight line or turning on the radio and singing a song. I imagine myself on stage, reading through my book's manuscript, finding the holes and sections that don't make sense. Truer sustained play involves more engagement than playful actions, but they are the stepping stones to building a more playful life.

We must be careful to draw a line between play and entertainment. While entertainment serves as a nice distraction that can also provide a mental break from the exhaustion and stress of daily life, it does not serve the same function as play. We rely on entertainment as a poor substitute for play in the same way that we rely on caffeine to make up for our lack of sleep. When we are entertained, we are passive. Play is an active, engaged, creative sort of flow.

I'm convinced that much of the battle over play—the need to defend it as a reasonable activity for young children, and the desire to cut play as a means to achieving greater and grander academic success—is actually a symptom of cultural play deprivation. We cut our ties with our former child-selves too precisely and too cleanly, and we are hurting from a deep need to reclaim some of the possibilities we encounter through play.

Building First Language Programs

Two-year-old Sadie was shopping at the grocery store with her mother when the two passed a table with sample packets of dishwashing powder. Sadie, thinking she was missing a snack, began to point back toward the table, crying and flailing in the cart. Her mother responded, "Use your words."

Three-year-olds Eduardo and Taylor were working together to build a block tower when their two-year-old peer, Fran, took some of the blocks away. Taylor was furious and hit Fran to try and get the block back. Everyone was in tears when their child care provider arrived. "Taylor, you must not hit Fran. Use your words."

Four-year-old Ben was running down the sidewalk toward the park when he fell and scraped his knees. "Ouch. That hurts," said his teacher. "Let's go get a bandage." The two walked toward a bench at the park, Ben crying the whole way. When they reached the bench and sat down, Ben began telling his teacher—through mumbled and heavy sobs—about the incident. "You'll have to stop crying and use your words. I can't understand you."

These examples are commonplace, and the phrase "use your words" is ubiquitous in early childhood settings. But, as surprising as it may sound, there was a time in history when children were not asked to "use their words." Children were expected to be compliant and quiet, and if they were crying or misbehaving, they were expected to change their behavior, not "use their words" to supply the backstory for the misbehavior. Psychologist Haim Ginott is one pioneer who offered a different kind of adult–child communication model with his important research in the 1960s. In his work he urges parents to listen to their children, to encourage their children to talk about their feelings. "An interested observer who overhears a conversation between a parent and a child will note with surprise how little each listens to the other. The conversations sound like two monologues, one consisting of criticism and instructions, the other of denials and pleading" (2003, 11). Ginott provides alternatives, helping parents understand how to listen to children's feelings with respect. When children hit, for example, he advises that parents say, "If you are angry, tell it to me in words." He advocates clear and consistent boundaries while providing children outlets to manage their strong feelings.

Since Ginott's work, the phrase "use your words" has morphed into a kind of disinterested, generic response to a child's strong emotional experiences. Often the phrase lacks genuine empathy and instead communicates a distance or disapproval, a requirement that children articulate—in the language of adulthood—their experiences. Children can end up feeling defeated and unheard, lacking the tools to communicate verbally in the midst of a heated moment of anger, frustration, disappointment, or jealousy.

Helping children learn to communicate verbally is an important element of early years education, and children will have an easier time getting their needs met if they use socially expected ways to communicate those needs. At the same time, studying the culture of childhood requires a different approach. The cultural language of childhood is not a way to measure the child's ability to use the adult system of spoken language; it is, rather, an inquiry into the child's system for making meaning and expression, reclaiming some of the heart of Ginott's approach, which was fully fixed on the child's experience.

In my move to Switzerland, I had many opportunities to experience what it might be like to be a child with limited language abilities. When I went to the dentist for the first time, I was nervous. I could not speak French; what if my dentist did not speak English? Frankly, I'm not a big fan of the dentist even without a language barrier, but toss in the inability to understand the doctor, and I was on edge. When he entered the room to begin the exam, he opened with a string of French. I caught a few words, but mostly just stared like a deer caught in headlights.

After a few moments of speaking he smiled. "English?" he asked.

"Yes," I replied, relieved. What a relief to connect with someone who could speak my language, especially when my emotions were heightened and the situation felt scary. For me, French is difficult enough if I am in the safety of my quiet kitchen, listening to online lessons and repeating phrases. When emotions are high—when I am nervous about a painful tooth—my ability to practice my new budding language skills flies out the window.

What must it be like to be a child, caught in a flurry of strong emotions and incapable of communicating to a trusted caregiver? New verbal language skills take time to grow, and even after children are able to form sentences and describe their feelings in moments of calm, those abilities might disappear when facing the intensity of strong emotions. What would change if we began to communicate with children in their language of play instead of demanding that they communicate with us in our language? What if we used *their* words? The result would be authentic, play-rich programs, programs I am choosing to call "first language programs."

Let me share a story of four-year-olds André and Julio. They generally played well together, but over the course of one particular week, each interaction was antagonistic.

"That's my car!" yelled André.

"No! It's mine!" responded Julio.

"Fine! Then I'm *not* going to play with you!" screamed André, who broke into sobs and threw his car at Julio.

My typical solution to problems like this was to sit on the floor with the children and process the disagreement. "Sounds like you two are angry. We can solve our problems, and I can help. It sounds like you both want the car. How can we solve that problem? I know. Maybe Julio would like a turn. Then André? Okay. Sounds like we came up with a plan." I tried this strategy for a week and it brought only short-term relief before the two resumed arguing.

One morning, I tried speaking their language. I sat near the boys as they bickered, and picked up two cars. Without mention of the fight, I began circling the cars around on the ground. *"Vroom, vroom.* I'm the fastest car. No, I am. Wanna race?" I talked for the cars. Then, I looked up at the boys. "What we need is a racetrack. You can build it with me if you want. Then we can drive fast. I'm going to get the racetrack."

André's sobs stopped immediately, and both boys sat frozen, watching me walk to fetch the racetrack. When I returned, I began linking the flexible orange track into a long line and I invited the boys to give their input. "We should have this track go over a mountain. Do you two want to find some blocks we can use for a mountain?" The three of us worked together building a racetrack, the boys offering their suggestions and assuming more and more control over the script. I backed away, yielding the lead to their collective imaginations. I never mentioned the argument, but spent the morning close to André and Julio and listened to their play.

Before I go further, I want to be clear that I think it is critically important to help children learn specific problem-solving strategies, and I don't think distracting children from a problem is ever the best solution. But this is not an example of distracting; the fact that the boys were fighting over toys was actually a symptom of a desire to play and an inability to create a collective script. The solution was not an adult-language-rich problem-solving process, but a culturally relevant play-based response. When I began to speak with them in their language, we built a foundation for the two to successfully construct their own imaginary world again. Outside the moment of the argument, we talked about ways to handle problems with friends, but in that particular moment, speaking in their language was the best way to help them recover their footing. In part, building first language programs allows us to take the play of children seriously by allowing *play* to be the primary vehicle for working through problems. Rather than suspending the play script to dialogue about problem solving and solutions, we can remain within play to repair friendships.

Characteristics of Children's Play

The language of childhood has certain characteristics, and understanding those characteristics will help us as we attempt to create first language programs.

Continuity

The first characteristic of children's play language is its continuity. A typical day for a child is like a symphony—one piece of music divided into individual movements, but connected with an unbroken theme. For children, there is continuity across meals and playtime, and they are capable of persisting in character and with integrity to the script if allowed. This desire for continuity is some of the reason why transitions are so difficult for children. Transitions are fundamentally disorienting, and yet most early childhood education environments are full of transitions. Morning welcome, breakfast, reading time, outside time, sensory play, music and movement, centers, free-choice play, cleanup, and lunchtime pack our schedules with tiny incremental moments of adult-orchestrated play.

In first language programs, we work to maintain sameness across the hours. In the story that opened this chapter, the mud puddle remained outside, but we continued to talk about it, share stories about it, draw pictures of it, tell fictional accounts of similar mud puddles, bring mud and clay into the art area, sing songs about it, and write letters to parents about it. We maintained continuity through play. Just because we closed the door to the physical outside does not mean we also had to shut down the play. By maintaining some continuity, we help prevent a kind of psychological whiplash that accompanies the feelings of being pulled out of a script.

Continuity is an important theme for children of all ages, especially for babies, who sometimes appear like props in the unfolding drama of daily child care life. From feedings to diapering to sleeping to playtime, young infants, without intentional and thoughtful care providers, may experience their days as a series of passive truncated events in which they are moved from one to the next based on the whim and availability of adults. Fortunately, there are some simple strategies to help babies experience continuity, as seen in the following stories of high-quality care.

Young Carter, four months, lies near a window, gazing at the tree outside. His care provider, Bee, notices he needs a new diaper. She moves in close to Carter and follows his gaze with her eyes, taking care to make her presence known before speaking so she doesn't startle him out of his moment. "You are looking out that window. I see a breeze blowing the trees. I wonder if it is warm or cold outside. I can tell you need a new diaper." At this point, she can secure eye contact with Carter, if she doesn't already have it, asking, "Can I pick you up to go change your diaper?"

By moving slowly, bringing her presence gently alongside Carter, she limits the effects of her interruption. She affirms that what he is doing is significant. By asking for permission before moving Carter out of his space, she affirms the idea that he is in charge of his body. And while he can't offer a verbal response at this point, babies who grow up with this style of interaction from birth very quickly learn to give physical cues to care providers as an answer to their questions.

Often, in our attempt to build language, we spend whole days talking, and while speaking with children is critical to their development, sometimes using the language of childhood involves no speaking at all. Active Senia, seven months, props herself on her hands and knees in a crawling position and shifts her weight forward and backward repeatedly. She plops back onto her belly, lifts her hands and feet off the floor, and waves them as if swimming laps in an imaginary pool. She maneuvers back onto her hands and knees and repeats the same series over and over again. Care provider Daniel observes this precrawling with enthusiasm. Senia has always been an eager explorer, and the thought of the joy she will experience with mobility makes him smile. He sits nearby and observes silently, his presence affirming what she is doing without the need for language to detract from her experience.

As children grow, so does their capacity for depth and duration. Play scripts that begin in the morning have the potential to stretch on for days, and children need help to protect these deep explorations from becoming the collateral of the fractured nature of adult-driven schedules. First language programs resist imposing unnecessary transitions and, instead, allow children's interests and passions to lead the direction of every day. Educators think critically before requiring that children stop the tasks they are pursuing in order to move to a new area. Is it necessary for all children to do art every day? Is it necessary for all children to participate in story time? Rather than enforcing uniformity, educators in first language programs ask questions of the program structure.

There will be numerous unavoidable transitions, and educators can teach strategies so children can return to their places with limited disruption. When I write, I highlight portions of my text so I know where to return the next day. This quick visual note pulls me back to my previous work session so that I find less of a delay when I have to start and stop.

Children benefit from their own versions of this place-holding technique, and providing them with tools and resources to save their place communicates a very important message: *I see what you are doing, and it is important.* Some potential tools and resources include the following:

> **Written notes or audio recordings.** Children can be encouraged to write notes or make audio recordings as a way of reminding themselves about what they were doing. Some children write a sticky note with their name as a way of identifying items still in use. Others will ask for help dictating a

note for the following day that can be left in their cubby. "I was playing zoo with Megan. We were going to do our exercises." Still others find that making an audio recording allows for greater depth and detail. "We were playing king and queen. Aleja, Ruby, Ahn, and me were playing. Aleja was wearing the red dress. Ruby was wearing the yellow vest. There was a fire dragon hiding to try and attack the castle. Ahn and me were standing guard. We were wearing guard hats and boots."

A "save-it" table. When I began my family child care program, my mentor, Kelly, shared an idea from her program that was enormously helpful. The children she worked with used a "save-it" table to protect objects in use during short transitions such as breaks to use the bathroom, getting a drink of water, or finding a sweater. This spot encouraged children to take necessary breaks (particularly bathroom breaks) without worrying that their objects would be taken by other peers.

Recording images. A tower that must be dismantled in between work sessions can be saved on paper by drawing a model of that tower. Educators can introduce this idea by making models of children's work during observations.

Photography. In addition to written maps and models, digital photography opens the possibility for a different kind of continuity, particularly between the child's home and child care spaces. Once, a child in my program was sobbing at departure time because he desperately wanted to take home a bucket of worms that he had collected with a peer during the day. A photo made this impossible request possible: "You wish you could take the worms home. I can't let you take them home, but I can take a picture of them for you and send it to your family. Then you could share your story about the worms at home, and remember where they will be when you come back tomorrow."

One of the more difficult aspects of incorporating these place-saving techniques into child care environments is that they take time. In order to allow children the opportunity to make models, write notes, or take photos, we have to plan extra buffering time around the transitions. Introducing these ideas well outside of the moments of transition is critical; knowing these strategies are possible will help children accommodate the idea of an upcoming transition.

Objects of Play

Early childhood programs are full of imitations—a play kitchen stocked with plastic food, a dramatic play area filled with commercially designed play clothes, baby board books with pictures of people. Everything must be easily sanitized. Even the utensils and dishes children use at mealtimes are typically plastic versions of the real thing. Often, the underlying fear is one of safety: if children have real, adult objects, then they will hurt themselves or others. Real glass can be broken. Real tools can cause damage. Babies who aren't protected (in swings and bouncy seats) might get stepped on. Implicit in this plastic world is the message that the pursuits of childhood are just imitations of real life—insignificant and to an extent fake.

First language programs make a point of including real tools. Children who are allowed to play with real objects use those objects to do real work. This is why children don't want to use the toy broom as much as they do the real broom, why the toy hammers are not nearly as enticing as the real hammers, and why babies spend far longer interacting with the real people in their environment than they do the mobile with pictures of faces. With all real objects, educators must take care to introduce tools in responsible ways—with adequate supervision and in settings when children are capable of developing mastery. Educators must also teach children the proper use of safety equipment such as eye protectors and hard hats. In preparing to stock your classroom with real objects, consider shopping in nontraditional places like hardware or thrift stores.

Play areas	Options for real objects
Dramatic play	stethoscopes, bandages, broom and dustpan, hats, vests, doctor/ nurse scrub shirts, pots and pans, real dishes (lightweight and break resistant), cloth napkins
Science and math	magnifying glass, microscope, glass eyedroppers, real tools like hammers, screws, nuts and bolts, screwdrivers, real wood to use in building, desk calculator with paper ribbon, wood blocks, mirrors, prisms, magnets
Outdoor area	clay bricks for building, real shovels and garden tools, wood stumps, sticks
Reading center	reference books like atlases, cookbooks with full-color pictures, photography books with pictures of real animals and people
Music and movement	any instruments can be real: tam- bourines, maracas
Art	real scissors, hole punches, beauti- ful fabrics, artist-quality paints and brushes
Infant spaces	objects with different textures for mouthing like large wooden rings, mirrors positioned low on walls, col- orful glass hanging in the windows

Repetition

Predictability is empowering. When I was in my midtwenties, my partner and I packed a moving van in California and drove to our new home in Iowa City for graduate school. I was born and raised in the same home in California. I attended college twenty miles away. After graduation, I stayed in the same area and continued to live and work in the same thirty-mile radius. Our first weeks in Iowa City were exhilarating. I developed a new grocery shopping routine and found the farmers' market. We located new restaurants and shopping centers for home improvement projects. My partner began graduate school, and we developed a fluency with the city bus system. But I remember one particular afternoon, about a month after we moved. I was driving home from a shopping trip, and I could not remember the directions. I pulled over and consulted a paper map in my glove compartment and cried. I longed for the day when my new city would feel familiar, when I wouldn't need a map to make it home from Target, when I had friends and knew where to go out to eat. I knew to give myself time; it had only been a month. And still, I felt exhausted from the constant newness.

In time, Iowa City became a home, but I have never forgotten those first weeks of orienting. It took me time to learn the most direct route between one place and the next, find the best place to shop for a variety of different foods, and discover the forest paths and walking trails that the residents enjoyed. Staying in Iowa City for a while freed my mind from the need to focus on directions.

This is the culture of childhood, and we have to remember that children look at repetitious experiences through a different lens. Repetition is not boring, and paradoxically, repetition can actually free children to experience novelty. Unlike their adult care providers, children are not bored after the tenth reading of *Goodnight Moon*. Through each successive reading, their minds are free to attend to something new. Perhaps they notice the sound of the turning pages during the first reading. Then, after the turning pages lose their allure, they notice a link between the pictures on each page and the sound of the words that accompany those pictures. In subsequent readings, they notice the colorful drawings that follow the black-and-white ones, or they wait with anticipation for the cow that jumps over the moon, or the sound of the lady whispering *hush*, or they notice the mouse that appears in every scene. As adults, we get bored with reading the same books over and over—and rightly so! We have ceased to be awed by the sound of a turning page, and with finely tuned phonemic awareness skills, we are no longer amazed at the magical synchronicity of words and pictures. If these experiences remained novel and compelling, no one could make it through the introduction to this book! But understanding the culture of childhood means appreciating the function of repetition in its cultural context.

One of the practices of my in-home child care program was to design the daily agenda collectively as a group at breakfast. I often brought ideas and materials to spark the interest of the children, but creating the list remained entirely in their hands. The lists would typically consist of activities such as walking to the park, building with blocks, and playing a game of zoo or kings and queens. Before long, I noticed that each day's new list was very often a duplicate of the one that came before.

Not all novelty is bad. Children get excited about new experiences, field trips, books, and materials. But we must question the frequency with which we change the routine for our children. Whether consciously or not, we tend to take a "checklist" approach to learning, supported by the adoption of state standards. These standards separate each domain of learning and articulate milestones. So, I can look up the motor development of infants and toddlers and see that they are supposed to be mastering the pincer grip. As a teacher, I can arbitrarily decide that today will be "Pincer Grip Thursday." I can design all kinds of activities to build and strengthen the pincer grip—sticker play, play with clothespins, or water play with turkey basters and pipettes. When the parents arrive, I can write down, "Today, we worked on standard 2.3" and describe the success their children had with their fine motor skills. Then I can check standard 2.3 off my mental list and move on.

There is nothing wrong with identifying milestones or articulating standards to measure learning, but we can easily fall into thinking of the standards as a to-do list. We can mistakenly measure our own success by the quantity of standards we address in a day or a week. We inappropriately assume that the sum total of a child's learning is held within such checklists, and we feel a need to grow every domain of learning every day. We believe that children are smarter if they meet the standards more quickly, or in a time well beyond what is expected for their age. In standards-focused classrooms, the keys to learning are determined by the culture of adulthood. There is no standard that says that around the age of eighteen months, children will read *Goodnight Moon* ten times in a row, or that four-year-olds will want to take the same neighborhood walk to look for worms for three weeks straight. If we conceive of learning as a to-do list, there is no room for repetition because repeating an activity is the antithesis of checklist productivity.

Instead of viewing childhood learning as a checklist, we should start thinking about it as an unfolding flower. The petals on the outside will be the first to unfold, and if we try to push them too quickly, they will bend and break. As a teacher, if you suggest an idea and it doesn't gain any traction, have the courage to set it aside for another time. If the children are deeply engaged in what they are doing—even if it appears to be the same thing they did yesterday and the day before and the day before that—boldly let it continue. Instead of setting up four different learning stations for one morning, set up one. Children, through their behavior, will let us know when they are satisfied and ready for something else.

Children don't need exotic adventures; each day in and of itself overflows with "new." To an infant, "new" may be the feel of her car seat buckle, the flash of light reflected from the kitchen window and onto her knee, or the sound of a dog barking as the mail carrier passes. To a toddler, "new" may be an automatic flush toilet, water that miraculously and ceaselessly flows from the bathroom faucet, or the crash of a glass hitting a tile floor. To a four-year-old, "new" may be recognizable letter combinations in books and on store signs, the feel of swinging on the monkey bars, or a friend who decides not to play. Educators in first language programs trust that repetition is a key element of early years learning, and they resist the urge to constantly change activities unless other signals indicate the need to move to something new.

Trust

Ultimately, building programs that value the first language of childhood relies on trust, but that is not always a simple proposition. "Trust in children as learners," observe educators Elizabeth Jones and Gretchen Reynolds, "is even less easily acquired than trust in oneself as a teacher" (2011, 6). In a society that strips children of agency through a continuum model of human development, children have no ability to be agents in their own learning. But, as we insist on children's rights as full human beings, we trust in their language of play as a foundational element of their existence. In developing programs that honor the first language of children, we are free to trust that the activities children naturally select on their own are the exact experiences they need to create meaning in their world. In such programs we think deeply about the times we interrupt and distract children from their pursuits. We take the scripts of young children seriously, resisting our urge to laugh at or belittle their ideas as cute or quaint. In first language programs, we trust that giving children real tools helps them do real work.

For communication to take place between two parties, they have to have a common language. And, beyond simply understanding dictionary definitions, both parties need to have a common cultural awareness for the meaning to transmit appropriately. The vocal inflections, the intentional pauses, the volume of speech, and the nonverbal elements are all clues to the overall meaning of a conversation. Children need adult outsiders who will commit to learning their language of play, and build programs that support their communication skills.

When children are engaged in play, we will not interrupt. When children struggle to play with their peers and it might be easier (and quicker) to distract them into a separate pursuit entirely, we will not overrule. When children are having a hard time doing what we want them to do, we will not use the language of play to try and manipulate their behavior, as sometimes happens when we play games to get children to clean up quickly. When children arrive in the morning, we will not dictate their scripts. Instead, we will maintain a posture of openness and trust as children grow, seeking to support their play as we do their spoken language development.

Stories from the Field

THE VALUE OF FENCELESS PLAY

by Denita Dinger

The cross-contamination of toys used to make my head buzz. If a book had somehow wandered away from the "Book Nook" and was in cahoots with a block in the "Building Zone," my pulse would quicken.

I spent the majority of my day scootching toys back to where they "lived" all while *trying* to calmly say, "Boys and girls . . . the blocks belong in the Building Zone" (insert overly sweet, sing-songy voice in attempt to hide my quickening pulse).

Why did I feel the need to keep the toys from migrating together? Did I think some horrid hanky-panky would occur if the blocks were allowed to mingle with the play food? Did I think the room would become so incredibly messy that the children and I wouldn't be discovered for days and make the headline on the national news?

No. Of course not. I was afraid of what the *parents would think*. I put the parents' expectations in front of what was best practice for the children.

I was a family child care program that touted itself as a "preschool program with wrap-around care." I *had* to look professional, and at the time, professional to me meant a neat and orderly environment where there were clearly marked learning areas.

I wanted parents to walk into my program and think, "Wow . . . I never knew family child care could be like this!" I wanted parents to know, without a doubt, that the children did waaaay more than "just" play while they were in my program.

I also thought young children were capable of learning about invisible boundaries and it would teach them responsibility and self-control if they had to be aware of where they were in the play space and where the toys were to be played with.

I am happy to report that, after years of transition and baby step after baby step, the toys in my program are now welcome to be played with anywhere. There are still play areas, but they are unfenced play areas.

What has happened since the liberation of toys in my program? Children "wonder if . . ." more. They wonder what will happen if we use the blocks as play food? Children create theories and test them. Along the same lines as wondering if . . . , after they discover the answer to their "wonder," they then test that theory with more materials. Children sit down and read books more. No longer trapped in the "Cozy Corner," books are now in baskets all over the play space. There are literally books everywhere *and* there is a safe home for books everywhere, so children can easily learn about respecting books by putting them away when they are finished.

Children's play is *free*! The fenceless environment allows for completely free exploration so the child can focus more on the play, rather than the worry of "can I play with this here?"

As for me? I am now free to carefully observe the beauty, wonder, and meaningful learning that are found in child-led play. I am now free to support the play my littles are leading without a worry of where the toys are, and how they got there. I am now free to work on quality relationships with each child.

Denita Dinger spent sixteen years as a family child care provider, and most recently operates Kaleidoscope Play School. For the past six years she has traveled across the United States and Canada keynoting early childhood professional conferences and leading one- to two-day trainings all focused on outside-the-box, open-ended play experiences as well as making the transition from a teacher-controlled program to one in which children are empowered to lead their learning through play. She has coauthored three books for Redleaf Press: Let Them Play: An Early Learning (Un)Curriculum, Let's Play, *and* Let's All Play.

CHAPTER FOUR

"It's Going to *Eat* Me!"
Systems of Belief

*"Humans develop their understanding of the world through the stories
that they share."*

—Steven Popper

*"What if one time, the bus went all the way up to the sky, and when it
got to our 'partment, we push the button, and go out of the door, and
jump onto the roof, and down, down, down, and into our 'partment?
[pause, staring wistfully out the window] That would be super."*

—Desmond, age three

THE FACT THAT CHILDREN HAVE RICH CAPACITIES for imagination will
not come as any surprise to those in the field of early childhood education. Spend the morning in an early childhood environment, and
you're bound to witness a parade of animals, an emergency trip to a
doctor to fix a broken foot, a group of firefighters putting out a fire, or
a cardboard box castle full of kings, queens, and servants. One of my
favorite snapshots of imagination occurred one morning after breakfast. I was washing the hands of a nine-month-old in his high chair
when I heard a knock at our door. I leaned over to see a good friend
and fellow child care provider arriving with her group for a morning of
shared play. We locked eyes and smiled, and I waved her in.

When she opened the door, there was an elaborate stage set by three
children—blankets covering the floor, baskets turned into baby beds,

pillows, children in elaborate costumes, and trays of pretend food. She crouched down by the group and greeted them.

"Good morning," she said to the children.

"Good morning," they replied.

"Would you go tell Emily that we are here to play?" she asked.

"We can't," said one of the boys. "We're on an airplane."

Young children believe in monsters. They believe in magic, flying spaceships, and the chance that one day, they might become unicorns. They believe that when they lose a tooth, a tiny fairy exchanges it for money, and that if they set out a plate of cookies in December, an old man dressed in a red velvet suit will slide down their chimney to leave presents. They want to be dolphins when they grow up, or superheroes, or fire trucks. As adults, many of us can recall fantastic dreams and beliefs from our childhoods, having heard the stories recounted by our families. "Remember when you said you wanted to be a butterfly when you grow up?" "Remember when you cut wings out of paper so you could fly?" "Remember when you thought you were a dinosaur?"

The belief system of childhood comes to life through their imaginative play, and often, the culture of adulthood looks to the belief systems of childhood as evidence of a sweet innocence that caricatures our understanding of children. Children believe in fantastic and magical worlds, and imagination is fascinating. As we observe children fully immersed in the rhythm of make-believe, we admire their creative thinking and flexibility. We are awed by their complex factual knowledge of specific real-life things—like airplanes—and the way this knowledge shapes their language use. We are amazed at their ingenious repurposing of materials to serve their imaginary scripts.

Childhood beliefs are powerful, and as long as they remain rooted in a sort of pretend realism—zoo, family, or airplanes—we don't give their belief systems much of a second thought. But their make-believe is not always so sanitized; zoo animals hunt one another, family members die with a strange matter-of-fact regularity, and airplanes crash. These untamed beliefs rattle us, and we wonder who is responsible for this scary twist in the plotline. We blame environment or media or contact with poor role models, but we never assume that the natural, uncontaminated well of childhood imagination contains both light and dark. We fear the implications of children's dark beliefs: that make-believe violence is somehow desensitizing, that scripts of death and revival confuse the finality of death, that play with violence limits the possibilities for constructive problem solving.

We don't understand the magnetic desire of children who appropriate the undesirable qualities of cartoon characters and animate them in their play, children who breathe life into the fearsome villains from their television worlds, or children who exhibit an insatiable craving to pretend to shoot one another with guns. Out of a strong desire to preserve the innocence in our early childhood environments, we ban the wild, violent, or scary elements and redirect imaginary play to the tame and domesticated storylines that aren't so problematic.

The systems of belief of childhood are rich and varied. Let's explore the basic structure of the child's belief system, and then, instead of sticking to the gentle, manicured path of fantasy, examine the wild and overgrown fringes of childhood make-believe, the dark forests that usually drive adults away: fear, violence, and scripts with "good guys" and "bad guys." Fasten your imaginary seatbelts!

Systems of Belief

Belief systems are the mechanisms we use to explain our understandings of the world. The culture of adulthood in America is characterized by a strong belief in rational thought. Logical, scientific, and empirical explanations for natural phenomena are highly valued. Anything that can't be proved is dismissed as superstition. American culture makes some exception for religious beliefs (as long as those beliefs aren't too far removed from the beliefs of the majority), but even these accepted beliefs are often disparaged as resembling a mythical belief in Santa Claus. This literal belief system doesn't make much room for emotion or feelings. Making decisions by "trusting your gut" is often considered foolish. Individuals who are rational and logical are more "civilized" than those who are highly emotional or cling to unfounded belief systems in the face of contradictory evidence.

Belief in the culture of American adulthood varies widely from the belief systems of other cultures around the world, as well as differing greatly from the belief systems of childhood. In 2014, while our family was traveling with Semester at Sea, we spent a few days in the port city of Kochi, in southwest India. One evening, my daughter spotted a gecko on a stucco wall in a small alley. Reptile aficionado that she was, she readied herself for a lightning-fast catch, and a few tense seconds later, she proudly showed off the tiny lizard to her brother and sister. From down the street, one of the local shopkeepers began to yell at us in a long string of Hindi punctuated with accented English, *"Poison! Danger!"* She released the gecko, surprised at the sudden attention her action had garnered. Later that evening when we returned to our cabins on the ship, we read about geckos and, specifically, the beliefs of some Indian and other Asian cultures. What we discovered was surprising. Geckos, though harmless, were believed to be poisonous.

Think about what you believe. Can you catch a cold from inadequate dress in cold weather? Are television screens bad for your eyes? Does cracking your knuckles lead to arthritis? Your beliefs will shape your behavior in a number of ways. Sometimes scientific facts can nudge these deeply held beliefs, but often, our belief systems determine which set of facts to hold and which to disregard. Consider more contested topics such as climate change, vaccines and autism, or sleep-training methods for infants. Depending on your beliefs, you might refer to a different canon of research than someone holding an opposing view.

The belief systems of the culture of childhood often stand in opposition to the belief systems of adulthood. Rooted in fantasy and make-believe, children are characterized, in part, by their lack of scientific minds. The culture of adulthood holds two opposing views about the beliefs of childhood. On the one hand, a child's ability to believe is viewed positively by adults: it is a mark of their innocence, something we adults strive to protect through traditions like the tooth fairy or Santa Claus. There is a kind of cultural grieving that accompanies a child's move from innocence to knowing, and we do what we can to stop that move from happening too soon. We collectively mourn the commercialization of childhood, decry sexualized role models for young children, and fear the early onset of puberty in girls and boys. Adult culture values the aspects of childhood that maintain a sense of naïveté. On the other hand, our appreciation for the belief systems of childhood stops as soon as those beliefs move from innocent to untamed. Untamed beliefs are evidence of a kind of knowledge from which we think children should be protected, knowledge we don't think children should have. Children shouldn't experience death, violence, and hate, and when they do have encounters with these "adult" categories, we become worried. As long as children are playing zoo and family, we admire their play abilities. But the moment those scripts turn violent, we block them to "protect" the innocence of childhood.

The beliefs of childhood are important, not just because they are cute or noteworthy, and certainly not because they are a reminder of the child's innocence, but because they belong to the child and represent the way the child is interpreting the world. Just as unaware tourists might disrespectfully try to dismantle what they consider to be false beliefs in a new culture they're encountering, unaware adults often try to dismantle the false beliefs of childhood. We block violent play under a banner of zero tolerance, and we refuse to take children's fears seriously. Instead, as culturally aware outsiders, we must recognize the beliefs of childhood as marks of humanity, observing with respect the role these beliefs play in the child's interpretation of the world.

Rich emotional lives play out in the make-believe of young children. If we begin to recognize and accept the full emotional experiences of our young ones, it will come as no surprise when their play themes represent both good and bad. Memories of my own make-believe are vivid and dark—babies that died, evil witches who chased me through dark forests, and bad guys who stole what I needed to survive. I know these dark themes were not the only images I played with as a young child, and even now as an adult, I admit that if those themes surfaced among the children in my care, I might wonder: Where did that come from? Did she see something inappropriate on television? Has she experienced some kind of trauma? Did she spend time with an older sibling or friend who told her things she couldn't understand? I would pay more attention to a story line involving dying babies than I would to a group of children politely camping under imaginary stars. Our adherence to a narrow vision of childhood innocence makes us suspicious of make-believe worlds that include death, fear, sadness, and loss. Still, I remember crying real tears for those imaginary dead babies, feeling real panic at being lost in an imaginary forest, and sensing real urgency because my supplies were running out.

The power of fantasy in the culture of childhood is that it provides a safe place to test what it feels like to be angry, sad, scared, or powerful. We need to keep in mind that when we respond to beliefs, even wildly fantastic beliefs, we are responding to real feelings. Whether we intend to or not, the messages we send about a child's fictional play has consequences in his real life. When we disparage the contents of his play and demean the depth and emotion of his beliefs, we are sending messages to the child about his real experience. Despite the fact that their make-believe is not real, the beliefs of young children contain important truths. A child will not actually wield real magic when he dons the requisite costume and picks up his wand, but he will access real power in the context of his fantasy and imagine the implications of that power for his real life.

Understanding the culture of childhood requires that we reevaluate our understanding of the systems of beliefs children use. Fantasies that include dark and scary themes point to truths that are as significant as the safe, domesticated ones, and when we interrupt those fantasies, we block the child's ability to manage the big feelings of fear, power, and grief within the safe confines of make-believe. Says writer Mary Howarth:

> We do not limit the colors we offer [children] with which to paint; we
> encourage their experimentation with art media, enriching their envi-
> ronments with texture and shape. But we are often afraid to recognize
> that a child's life is made up of both light and dark feelings, which she

also needs to name and utilize. How can she know that humankind has experienced all these same feelings for millennia? (quoted in Jones and Reynolds 2011, 129)

Childhood Fears

Childhood fears have always been a source of mystery for adults. We remember what it was like to be afraid as a child, and we want to do what we can to prevent children from experiencing the same fears we had. Sometimes, children are afraid because their experiences make them afraid. They fear the doctor because they remember the prick from the last visit's shot. They fear the vacuum because they remember the noise it made when it was used last. But often, they are afraid of imaginary things or things that can't do them any harm: the dark, monsters, bugs, loud noises, dogs, bikes, squishy food, adults, thunder and lightning, bees, balloons—the list could go on and on. Fears are developmentally expected, and with age and life experience most children outgrow the frightening preoccupations of their early years. Still, these fears are consuming while children are experiencing them, and caregivers need ways to support children helpfully as they grapple with the unknown.

Colette grew up in my family child care program and developed an intense and powerful fear of flying bugs when she was two. I ran my program exclusively outside when the weather permitted, so her fears became an increasing challenge as the spring air warmed. What was I supposed to do when faced with a child suffering a real and debilitating fear?

Our modern cultural and scientific beliefs about fear often lead us to respond in one of two ways. The first is attempting to talk the child out of being afraid by convincing her that what she fears is fake. I call this "fictionalizing the fear." When we fictionalize the fear, we point out the ways in which the fear is not real. In Colette's case, I could tell her that flies don't hurt people. Likewise, we tell children that monsters are pretend, the closet is empty and benign, and the vacuum cleaner is incapable of sucking up a person. Our attempts to fictionalize the fear are genuine attempts to help. We care for children and we want to do everything in our power to erase the hold of fear in their lives. But fictionalizing a genuine emotion is dismissive and invalidating. Even if the fear is unfounded, the emotion is intensely real. I am afraid of sharks, and even though I know the likelihood of being bitten by a shark in the ocean is minuscule, I still have an intense emotional reaction when I swim. Logic is powerless to undo the chemical biological processes that are activated when the fear portion of the brain is triggered (Sunderland 2008). When a child who has been told by the most important adults in her life that her fears are not real still experiences real fear, she feels alone, overwhelmed, and ashamed of her out-of-control and "wrong" feelings. Children whose fears are consistently fictionalized by well-meaning adults will stop asking for help, rather than stop being afraid, knowing that their fears will be ignored or dismissed.

The second way adults try to help children is to *fix the fear*. When children are afraid of the dark, we plug in night-lights. When children are afraid of vacuums, we vacuum while they are away. When children are afraid of flying bugs, we bring out a flyswatter and swat the flies or we move our games inside. Children will find temporary relief, but our band-aid solutions don't offer long-term strategies to manage fear. Over time, fears change. Fears of the dark and monsters will be replaced in adolescence with fears of not fitting in or not getting into college, and those fears will be replaced in adulthood by fears of rejection, not making enough money, or living a life without meaning. Finding the resilience to face and challenge fears is an important step in developing lifelong skills for managing fear and anxiety. Every time we remove a child's fear, we interrupt an opportunity to help her learn to manage her fears.

Instead of fictionalizing or fixing the fears, we can offer strategies that help transform them. One strategy is to *imagine power* to counter the powerlessness of fear. This story, in which a five-year-old child was frightened of a character she had seen in a television show, demonstrates one such strategy. She was reluctant to stay on her cot at naptime, fearful of what would happen when the lights were turned off.

She and I cuddled together and we talked about the character. She began by saying, "I know it's not real, but every time I close my eyes, I see that monster."

I shared my own experience: "I know what it feels like to be afraid. When I'm afraid like that, I feel small and powerless. One of the ways you can ease your mind is to try to feel powerful again. Even though you know that monster isn't real, it feels real in your mind. Do you want to know what I do sometimes?"

"Yes."

"Well, if I know my imagination is making me feel afraid, then I can use my imagination to start to feel powerful again. Do you want to know what I would do if that monster walked in here right now?"

She responded with a fearful, but curious, "Yes."

"I would tie a magic balloon onto its wrist so it would float away. Or, I would put a magic spell on it and turn it into a dandelion, and then I would blow it into the wind. What would you do?"

"I would kick it with a super hard kick that would send it all the way to outer space."

"I would put a rocket under my cot. When it came close to me, I would stuff it into the rocket and fly it to the moon."

"I would blow magic bubbles that would surround it and it couldn't see and it would run all the way into the desert."

We continued like this for a while. When we had tapped our streams of consciousness, I said, in an effort to reassure her, "You may still feel frightened, but you can use your imagination to pretend something powerful, and that can help." It took time to cuddle with her and talk through these different ideas. The powerful images that she conjured were not fixes but rather strategies for managing an emotion that made her feel powerless.

A second strategy is to *help children develop a plan*. There are children for whom the mysterious is scary, and the lack of information leaves them feeling powerless. Right after our family had moved to Switzerland, my daughter went through a phase of questioning the different outcomes of scary situations. The questions usually started off plausible, but quickly became more extreme: "What would happen if the bus left and you got on, but I was left at the bus stop?" "What if we were all at the train station, and you and Daddy both fell on the tracks and got killed by a train?" "What if my little brother fell off a cliff while we were hiking?" "What if you died and left me alone at the top of the cliff? How would I get down?"

It was always tempting to say, "That's never going to happen," but her fears were rooted in the reality of not knowing, and as I answered her questions and took her seriously, she was able to develop a mental plan for gaining knowledge in a new environment. In addition to answering her questions, I helped her put together the plan. I wrote our cell phone numbers on an index card and laminated it for her backpack. I taught her our street address and street name, and some basic French so she would be competent in asking for help from a stranger. I showed her where to watch for our street name on the television monitor on the bus so she would know when our stop was coming. Even though I knew the chances that she would be left alone on a bus or out in the city with no adult to bring her home were infinitesimal, those minuscule chances did not matter. She wanted to have a plan.

There are many ways to help our children make plans:

Show them how to ask for help. This skill grows incrementally, starting with such skills as knowing how to ask for a towel when a child spills his milk or knowing how to ask for peers to assist in tower building. But it also includes emergency preparedness skills, like knowing how to find a neighboring teacher or adult if something happened to the primary care provider.

Use a daily pickup chart. Children should know who will be picking them up at the end of the day. Child care spaces can use pocket charts to pair a picture of the child with a picture of the person picking him up at the end of the day.

Ask, "What will you do today?" Morning gathering times (mine always happened over breakfast) are great times for making daily plans. Ask the children, "What will you do today?" They can think about what they would like to do and who they might do it with. Writing their ideas on a chart reinforces that their ideas will be taken seriously.

Prepare children for changes in the daily routine. Will you be painting or rearranging the child care space over the weekend? Prepare the children in advance. Will you be taking a field trip to the zoo? Prepare the children in advance. Will you be expecting a visitor? Prepare the children in advance. As much as possible, children should know what's happening every day.

A third strategy is to *give children chances to play with their fears*. Sometimes, children's fears grow out of life experiences, and they need time and tools to process the events that are frightening. This kind of play might manifest in subtle ways that adults might not notice, like games of mommy and daddy in which children test the experience of being in power. At other times, care providers intentionally structure environments that give fearful children chances to interact with their fears in safe and controlled ways. In Colette's case, I added books about bugs to the bookshelf and plastic bugs to the collection of toy animals. Providing children opportunities to play with the objects that make them afraid will help them learn how to categorize their fears.

One spring day, my family child care crew had a collective experience that left everyone feeling scared and unnerved, and I had the chance to put this practice of playing through fear to work. All the children were outside playing in the sand, enjoying the warm air that drew blankets of violets, dandelions, and clover over the rolling Iowa landscape. I sat in the sunshine sharing stories with my local home child care consultant, who was visiting my program that morning. We both watched as the children made birthday cakes out of sand, sticks, leaves, and grass, presenting to each other the gifts born out of time, materials, and endless creativity. It was idyllic.

One of the children picked up a rock and threw it at Jeanie, who was playing in the sand. The throw was friendly, part of the game, intended for good, and also very poorly aimed. Jeanie turned to me with blood streaming down her forehead, and my stomach turned. After some basic first aid (gloves, gauze, antibiotic ointment, bandage), I had to make *that* call to her parents: "I'm calling because Jeanie might need stitches. She's fine, and the bleeding has stopped, but the cut is on her forehead, and you will want to come and look at it. She might need to see a doctor."

I explained the context surrounding the gash, and I was lucky to have the help of another qualified adult to care for the group while I focused my attention on the injured child and her parents. I was also relieved to have the perspective of another early childhood professional to help me fill out incident reports. As the children lay down for their naps that afternoon, I felt shaky from nervous adrenaline. My primary responsibility was to keep the children safe, but despite my best efforts, someone had been hurt. I replayed the event over and over in my mind. I called some of my colleagues to share my story. I taught a class that evening to a group of home child care providers, and for the first ten minutes, we shared stories of dealing with accidents. I processed the event from every angle to evaluate my responses—I'm sure I even dreamed about rocks that evening. In telling and remembering my story, I was mentally assimilating this unsettling event into my mind, making sense of it and validating my own competence in spite of the unknown. It was because of this mental set of gymnastics that I was able to reopen the next day. My confidence was not destroyed, merely shaken. And it was through the retelling that I was released from the fear of future accidents.

At the doctor, Jeanie's family discovered that the cut required one stitch, which was a traumatic ordeal. For the rest of the children, the incident was still scary and unsettling the next morning. Blood, crying, phone calls to parents, another adult helping meet their needs while I was preoccupied—these were all a source of anxiety. The children were anxious for Jeanie to return the next day so they could examine the wound. When she appeared, everyone gathered around, and she told about her experience. For the morning that followed, and in the days and weeks that ensued, the children played stitches, where one child would dress as a doctor, one would dress as an injured child, and they would reenact the experience. Reflecting on my own process of working through a difficult experience, I made space for the children to do the same by adding medical props to the play area: adhesive strips, magnifying glasses, lab coats, an elastic bandage for sprains, stethoscopes, prescription pads, and a surgeon's regalia. We read stories about children at the doctor, wrote our own social story about the day Jeanie got stitches, and watched the healing of her forehead. The child who threw the rock was shaken; she had not intended to hurt Jeanie, and was unraveled by the scary string of events that followed her poorly aimed throw. She was cautious in the days that followed, alarmed by her own power. We had some conversations about safety and rocks, but, more important, we talked about how children can help each other when they are hurt and the fact that accidents happen.

When children are afraid, or when group experiences leave children feeling alarmed, consider the following ways to help them play with their fears:

- Provide books to increase familiarity with a subject while giving children control of how quickly to move with the subject.

- Add props to a sensory table, for example, small plastic bugs in the sandbox to give children experience with the subject of their fears while they are powerful and in charge.

- Script scenarios for children to practice. In the case of my daughter who was afraid when we arrived in Switzerland, we asked friends to talk with her in French so she could practice asking for help.

We must take children seriously. As educator Mary Howarth says, "What a relief it is for a child to find that the things she is worried about are taken seriously!" (Howarth 1989, 61). What relief, indeed! When we resist the urge to dismiss or fix the seemingly irrational fears of young children, they feel understood and validated in the core of their beings.

Children's Violent Make-Believe

The violent play of young children, by and large, makes early childhood educators nervous. I get it; it makes me nervous, too. The sight of young children pretending to shoot each other with pretend guns triggers our fears about the safety of our world, and calls to mind a mental newsreel of horrific events. As a society, we fear for the safety of our children, growing up in what we believe is a terrifying and dangerous world. But our fears are statistically unfounded (Mintz 2004; Holland 2003; G. Jones 2002; Mercogliano 2008). Though it seems hard to believe, the world is safer now than it has ever been. Rates of accidental deaths of children are down. Teen smoking, drinking, and pregnancy are all down. If children are safer than they have been, why are we so fearful?

The biggest reason was summed up by Lenore Skenazy, founder of a movement called Free-Range Kids, in a keynote address at an early childhood conference I attended in Canada in November 2013. In her comments, she termed this panic the "Google effect" (Skenazy 2013), which basically compares our minds to an Internet search engine. If we contemplate child dangers, our minds will recall everything dangerous we have ever read or heard about, irrespective of the likelihood. Another way to think of this generalized panic was aptly defined by Bruce Schneier, a computer-security expert, in a TED talk he delivered at Penn State University called "the security mirage."

> We estimate the probability of something by how easy it is to bring instances of it to mind. . . . If you hear a lot about tiger attacks, there must be a lot of tigers around. You don't hear about lion attacks, there aren't a lot of lions around. This works until you invent newspapers. Because what newspapers do is they repeat again and again rare risks. I tell people, if it's in the news, don't worry about it. Because by definition, news is something that almost never happens. When something is so common, it's no longer news—car crashes, domestic violence— those are the risks you worry about. (Schneier 2011)

What Skenazy and Schneier are talking about, this reality that human beings have a tendency to exaggerate improbable risks, takes an enormous toll on the ways we interact with young children. Their violent play makes us nervous because we worry about the dangerous world they are inheriting. Historian Steven Mintz suggests, "Children have long served as a lightning rod for America's anxieties about society as a whole. . . . Unable to control the world around them, adults shift their attention to that which they think they can control: the next generation" (2004, 340). Using children as justifications for our anxieties is unfair and inappropriate. We must have the courage to explore the violent play of young children with unbiased eyes, setting aside our emotional reactions to their play and trying to understand it from within.

One of the most common policies in the early childhood environment with respect to war and weapon play is a policy of "zero tolerance." No pretend guns allowed. No toy guns, no making a gun shape with your fingers, no building a gun shape with blocks, no biting a cracker into the shape of a gun, and under no circumstances are children allowed to pretend to shoot one another with these pretend guns. Typically, the prohibition of guns extends to other weapons and weapon play as well. No swords, no sticks wielded like swords, no laser death rays, no throwing snowballs and pretending they are firebombs. We draw a wide margin of safety around anything violent, or anything that could turn violent, and ban it. Aggressive play, rough and rowdy play, play in which children mimic cartoon characters—all of it is suspect, and all of it is discouraged, redirected, or outright banned.

Zero-tolerance policies stem from wanting to raise children who will grow into peaceful adults and to maintain environments that are free of injury and chaos. These intentions, while important, are not at odds with the war and weapon play of young children. As educator Steven Popper says, "In practice . . . the *style* of children's play (e.g. making and using pretend guns or swords, or make-believe chasing villains or shooting webs like Spider-Man) is focused on, rather than the *content* of the play. The *substance* or *theme* of the scenario . . . would not necessarily matter to a professional enforcing a blanket zero tolerance approach" (2013, 10). Viewing childhood as a culture means exploring the function of war and weapon play from within that culture. The substance, theme, and content of play all matter equally to, if not more than, the style of play. In the section that follows, we will explore the myths that drive our commitment to zero-tolerance policies, and explore other ways of interacting with children in their violent make-believe. Because these myths are all deeply engrained and impossible to explore thoroughly in a few pages, in the section titled "Resources by Chapter," I have included an annotated list if you are looking for further reading to expand your own understanding.

Myth Number 1: Media Violence Leads to Real Violence

The idea that watching violent television or movies or playing violent video games *makes* a person more aggressive is a claim that is rarely contested, but an actual scientifically supported link between media exposure and real violence is surprisingly difficult, if not impossible, to prove. Research studies exploring the impact of media on human behavior are highly problematic since there is often no way to control for the anxiety-provoking, artificial laboratory situations in which participants are observed (Fowles 1999). In a famous study, children were observed in a lab after a period of watching *Mr. Rogers' Neighborhood*, and were found to be more aggressive after the television exposure than before. Instead of media inducing the aggression, writer Gerard Jones offers this interpretation: "It more likely means that being made by a strange adult to watch television makes a child anxious or angry. I love Fred Rogers, but I suspect if I were forced to sit in a hard plastic chair in a strange room and stare at him when I'd rather be out playing, I'd act aggressively too" (2002, 35).

Surprisingly, researchers who study children in their homes or other natural settings are unable to find a link between media and real-life violence (Fowles 1999; Holland 2003; Jones 2002). The studies that do claim to find a link often do not have lengthy enough observation periods. After a period of watching violent cartoons or action-packed television shows, child viewers do exhibit a surge of aggressive behavior. They pretend to fight or shoot each other with guns, or mimic the other actions of the characters. But after a short spike in aggression, children return to a normal mental state, and often grow more focused, creative, and imaginative after their play (G. Jones 2002, 40).

Why does television remain suspect after a half century of research into its dangers has come up short? The United States is one of the only countries that persists in researching links between the media and real-life violence. Other countries have given up (Fowles 1999, 21). In short, television is an easy target. No one will line up behind television to defend its status as a public good. So when a sense of public safety is threatened, we can focus our vague fears on a single target that can't defend itself, thereby pacifying our fears so we can cope with the stresses of daily life. This does not mean early childhood environments should increase the media consumption of children in their care, or that children should be allowed to consume media that is targeted to an adult audience. It simply means that the link between real-life violence and media violence simply does not exist in the way we think it does.

Myth Number 2: Pretend Fighting Leads to Real Fighting and Real Injuries

Real fighting is a result of a conflict between peers, not a result of a play script. Accidents can happen when children are play fighting, but those accidents are surprisingly few and far between, though as educators, we overestimate the amount of fighting that is actually real. In studies, educators assume that 29 percent of play fighting turns into real fighting when in fact only 1 percent of play fights become real ones (Holland 2003, 28). This is significant, because if we think children are really fighting, we have a responsibility to intervene. Presumably, therefore, we are intervening far more frequently than we need to. Interruptions in play are a source of anxiety for children and anxiety leads to aggression. In the end, it is possible that some of the real aggression we see in early childhood settings is actually a result of our frequent interruptions rather than the child's choice of play themes. What would happen if we waited, pausing before we rush to stop a script that appears to be aggressive? What if we trusted the children's play to come to a resolution that allows them to cope with real-life issues without forcing our own resolution prematurely?

Frankly, the impact of pretend fighting on the climate of an early childhood setting might be positive. Children who have a chance to discharge feelings of anxiety and fear in the protected realm of play are less likely to lash out at peers in real life. Children who practice using their big body muscles are less likely to be injured by accident because they have refined their balance, coordination, and spatial sense. Children who work to sustain play with peers rely on self-regulation to make sure everyone wants to stay involved—*If I actually hit a friend in the course of play fighting, he won't want to play anymore and he'll stop playing, so I'll hold back to keep the play going*—and that empathy and self-regulation transfer into all other areas of the child's life.

No artificial teacher-led games or adult-driven activities set up the kinds of opportunities to practice self-regulation and empathy the way organically unfolding play does. Rough and wild play carries the unique ability to push children's self-regulation abilities further, and this is specifically true for boys. Self-regulation is not as urgent in tame scripts such as house or farm; however, wilder and more violent themes carry greater risk, demanding a higher level of awareness from all children involved. Contrary to popular opinion, there is a significant and ever-growing body of research that suggests children who engage in war and weapon play are *less* aggressive after playing than they were before. As educator Frances Carlson writes in her book *Big Body Play*, rough-and-tumble play "supports social skill development[;] this aggressive play style can actually *help reduce* physical aggression in the long term" (2011, 17). We must consider the potential benefits of the play before we ban it completely.

Myth Number 3: Children Who Rehearse Violent Solutions Lack Creative Problem-Solving Skills

Educators tend to think of "good guy/bad guy" narratives as simplistic, representing all heroes and heroines as virtuous and villains as wholly evil, devoid of any greater sense of morality. Steven Popper's intriguing exploration of superheroes and weapon play offers a different perspective: "Children absorbing such stories are faced with exemplars of the development and expression of good moral character, and also of what difficulties, temptations and blind alleys a person might face as he or she struggles to act with moral integrity" (2013, 87). In engaging in pretend violent play, children are wrestling with some of the deep human struggles of integrity, power, justice, and the capacity to choose what is right. All of these are the foundations for creative problem solving.

Conflict-resolution skills require creativity and imagination, and children who have the chance to develop these skills in their early years have a broader set of conflict-resolution skills as adults. Therefore, while educators worry about play themes, they should instead focus on play complexity. A farm script that maintains its predictable simplicity day after day, month after month, should be just as notable for educators as a script of good guys and bad guys who pretend to shoot each other day after day.

Myth Number 4: War and Weapon Play Is Unnecessary and the Risks Are Too High; There's No Harm in a Zero-Tolerance Approach

We have difficulty seeing benefits of war and weapon play, so we feel justified in banning it. Instead, as we begin to understand why children might feel compelled to engage with these types of scripts, perhaps we will feel justified in supporting this type of play through carefully designed limits to protect the emotional and physical safety of everyone involved. Banning weapon play serves only to pacify our adult fears of children growing up to become violent adults, but it has no grounding in reality. Most children who engage in war and weapon play benefit by deepened self-regulation and empathy. They develop skills of imagination and creativity that are actually the foundation of problem-solving and conflict-resolution skills. Children who have practice managing their strong and powerful emotions in the context of play turn out to be *less* violent; they have practice dealing with anger or rage and channeling those emotions toward something constructive, even if that "something" appears to our adult eyes to be destructive. It is important that adults not instigate war and weapon play with young children; children benefit from engaging in such play when it comes from their own imaginations. As adults, we should not actively seek to add violent themes or play to the worlds of young children, but we should think twice before reflexively banning it.

Establishing Guidelines for Children's "Violent" Play

The question, of course, is "How?" In supporting the child's drive to play with violent or difficult themes, we must develop guidelines that ensure the safety of every child. Not all children have a need or a desire to engage in war and weapon play; a thoughtful approach can address the needs of both players and bystanders.

Guideline Number 1: Everyone Involved Must Want to Be Involved, and a Strategy for Stopping the Game Must Be Clear and Respected

Conflict management during all types of play involves teaching children language to use when they don't want to play. Consider the following scenario:

Two four-year-olds were playing lion, a game that involved crawling, growling, clawing at imaginary roadblocks, and hunting zebras. They approached a cluster of other children huddled around a tub of building blocks, when all of a sudden, one of the lions (Edgar) pounced on the unsuspecting builder (José) and yelled, "RAWR!"

"Hey! Get off! *No*! You broke my house! *Elise!*" José began crying and calling for his teacher.

Edgar, still in character, responded, "You're my dinner!"

José was in tears and pushed Edgar back. Edgar seemed to think this was part of the game; the zebra was putting up a fight! Elise, the teacher in this classroom, arrived in time to block further physical contact, and sat down to help figure out what had happened. She told José to use very direct language with Edgar: "Stop! I'm not playing that game right now." She reminded Edgar that he could only hunt zebras who *knew* they were zebras. She helped him practice pitching the idea to José and asking him to play. First, she role-played the part of José with Edgar, and then she gave the two boys a chance to practice.

EDGAR: "José? We're playing lions. Do you want to play?"

JOSÉ: "In a minute. I'm finishing a house. Then I want to play."

EDGAR: "We need a zebra so the lions can eat."

JOSÉ: "I don't want to be a zebra. I want to be a lion."

EDGAR: "Okay. *Hey!* I've got an idea! Let's use the stuffed animals as the zebras!"

This scenario is reminiscent of the "poison meat eater" scenario from chapter 2. In both cases, the educators involved are able to support the rights of the child who is playing an aggressive game without stopping it completely, modeling a means of playing that honors all children involved. Outside of the rough play, educators must help children learn to recognize signs that players want to stop. These signs may be verbal (saying "Stop!" or "No!" or "Oww!") or nonverbal (crying, grimacing, pushing). Practice out of the moment helps children learn to recognize these signs.

Guideline Number 2: Avoid Prepackaged Commercial Toys Tied to Specific Characters

Often, play that centers on prepackaged scripts is narrowing. There can be only one Dora, one Lightning McQueen, one princess, one bad guy. In one instance in my family child care program, two girls fought over who would be the one pet platypus from a cartoon. When I suggested the idea of two, they both practically fell over. "Emily, there is *only one* platypus!" Early childhood programs that aim to be more accommodating of make-believe violence won't prevent media-based scripts from unfolding during play, but will intentionally choose generic, non-media-based toys. Early childhood educators should think carefully about their policy allowing children to bring toys from home. On the one hand, such toys often spark creative play and help children carry over a sense of belonging both to home and school. On the other hand, toys from home might communicate messages or encourage play themes to which educators—for good reason—are resistant.

Guideline Number 3: Props Should Serve a Variety of Functions

Writer and early childhood researcher Penny Holland recounts an incredibly illustrative story of the power of open-ended toys in relation to war and weapon play. The story involves a child named Darren who was consistently in trouble for his classroom aggression with peers and his desire to enact scripts full of pretend violence. At the start of the year, the school he attended followed a strict zero-tolerance policy, and Darren was in trouble constantly. Later in the year, the faculty at the school decided to see what would happen if they relaxed the zero-tolerance policy as a way of pursuing more child-led play. Holland, who was present as a researcher, kept careful notes on Darren's behavior. Initially, Darren's play was repetitive and simplistic; he and a friend ran around the classroom all day, every day, pretending to shoot each other over and over with simple pretend guns they had fashioned from blocks. In time, the construction element of the game became more complex, with Darren and his friend building more and more sophisticated guns.

One day, after several months of this behavior, Holland observed Darren disassemble his gun and reassemble it into electric paddles to shock a pretend victim back to life. A few weeks later, she watched Darren, clad in doctor's gear, pushing a patient around the classroom. He took the toy gun, disassembled it, and made it into a plate of food for his patient, who was recovering (Holland 2003, 40–41). Over time and with the freedom to explore, Darren was able to push beyond his simple script. He developed skills that allowed him to play collectively with other children—skills he didn't have when his days were full of prohibitions and consequences for his misbehavior. The new setting made it possible for Darren to be a successful, contributing member of the classroom society.

Guideline Number 4: Use Caution When Getting Involved

War and weapon play is powerful when it comes from the imagination of the child. Adults should not introduce violent scripts in the hopes of nurturing the kinds of skills that children can foster when they engage in war and weapon play. Similarly, adults should refrain from participating in children's violent play unless the adult role is less powerful than the child's role. Since children are often exploring themes of power, we have a responsibility to let them use that power in the context of play.

My son spent his days at an early childhood center when he was three, and each day when I brought him home, we spent the first several minutes of our reunion play fighting. He always initiated the rough-and-tumble play with joy and enthusiasm. "Mom? Can we wrestle?" followed by a playful, "I'm going to bite your arms off!!" or "I'm strong up to the sky!" growled through clenched monster teeth. I would always crumple onto the floor, "Oh no! A ferocious beast!" As his play continued, I followed his lead. I would offer my own protections. "Good thing I have my magic shield to block you!" to which he would counter, "I have my magic that can melt your shield!" From my perspective, it seemed perfectly logical that he would need this type of play to discharge any built-up anxiety he felt at school, reclaim a sense of power and agency, and reconnect with me. Following our wrestling sprees, we would go our separate ways: me to work on my writing, and my son to his room to play with his toys. Playing together was a powerful experience, primarily because he was in charge.

I hesitate to say that adults should never engage in violent play with young children because never joining the play might communicate attitudes of disapproval about the child's experience. If you are an educator who joins children in the play kitchen, eagerly eating an imaginary pizza-pickle-ice-cream cone, when you are invited to join in the aggressive play of young children, you should participate if you feel comfortable. Some educators don't want to play with the pretend war and weapon play of young children, and this is a perfect time to model for children what it means to draw boundaries around what you do and do not want to do. "I don't feel like playing right now, but we can play a different game later."

As educators, we have a responsibility to examine the beliefs that unsettle us. Historian Steven Mintz reminds us that "since we cannot insulate children from all malign influences, it is essential that we prepare them to deal responsibly with the pressures and choices they face. That task requires knowledge, not sheltering. In a risk-filled world, naïveté is vulnerability" (2004, 382). Support for the culture of childhood demands that we refuse to belittle their otherworldly beliefs. We must champion the rights of childhood beliefs to be more than simply "cute" or "charming." In doing so, we have the chance to accompany children as they develop complex understandings of power, justice, and their capacities to act with integrity.

Stories from the Field

WE KNOW THE DIFFERENCE

by Tom "Teacher Tom" Hobson

I had been teaching a class of three- to five-year-olds for over a decade before our school, Woodland Park Cooperative School in Seattle, Washington, decided we needed a class made up solely of five-year-olds for families who wanted an extra year of preschool before kindergarten. At our school the children make their own rules and their own community agreements, and each year, the younger children had come to the subject of weapons. Every year of my tenure, we had agreed, by consensus, to ban weapons, both real and pretend.

I've been part of these conversations for a long time, involving a lot of different children, and it always goes down more or less the same way. Someone proposes "no weapons," and everyone agrees.

Then I ask about pretend weapons. Someone says, "No pretend weapons." I then ask, "Why?" and someone answers that even pretend weapons are scary. We then agree that no one should be afraid in preschool and that's that. I often wondered if this rule was made simply because the kids believed it's what the grownups wanted, that we had expressed our anti-gun sentiments so clearly that the kids were just reflecting it back at us. Whatever the case, this was the status of weapons play at our school up to the advent of the new class for five-year-olds.

I'd anticipated that our weapons discussion with the older kids would go more or less the same way. As I'd expected, we banned weapons during our first week in class, but when I asked about pretend weapons, I was surprised by the response: "Pretend weapons are okay."

I asked, leadingly, "Aren't you worried some people will be scared of the pretend weapons?"

"We know the difference between real and pretend weapons, Teacher Tom." I probed and prodded, but if anything the group's conviction became stronger. All of them, boys and girls, agreed that pretend weapons were okay.

I'll be honest: I didn't like it. At any given moment, someone in the outdoor classroom had someone else in the crosshairs. And the play was *intense.* It was something that mostly happened outdoors, this weapons play. We start our days out there and I had several parents tell me that getting their child to school on time was a piece of cake compared to previous years because they didn't want to miss even a single minute of our shoot-em-up outside time. As one might expect, it was the boys who were most excited by our permissive gun rules, but there were also girls right in the middle of the action as well, usually without guns, opting more often than not for wands, which for all practical purposes were the same thing. I tried, in quiet moments, to get one of the girls or less enamored boys to admit to feeling afraid of the weapons play, only to be told, quite clearly, "No, I am not afraid."

This went on throughout the school year, ebbing and flowing. At one point the focus was on swords, but after Rex took home a nasty bruise on his back, the kids agreed they ought to ban "swinging weapons," both real and pretend, so we were back to "shooting weapons," and mostly guns. Children and adults objected at times to being "targeted," so we agreed that you may only "shoot" at people who you know are part of the game.

In truth, when I stepped back and really watched what was going on, as opposed to merely reacting, I saw much less shooting and much more running around with sticks of one kind or another. I heard much more discussion about "teams" (the requirement for joining any one team was to simply declare yourself a member and you were in) or specific roles within the games (bad guy, good guy, guard, ninja, and so on). I watched constantly for facial expressions that told me someone was in over his head or had lost himself in the game and forgotten he could say, "Stop!" I remained vigilant for things getting out of control, for someone too excited by the game, who appeared to be crossing the line between pretend and real, as had happened when Rex got his bruise.

But mostly I found myself remembering similar games I had played as a boy, running wildly, hiding, imagining myself as a cowboy then an Indian, a cop then a robber, a good guy then a bad guy. I knew the difference between real and pretend weapons, just as I knew that I wasn't really a cop or a robber. I remember that my mom didn't like it. She would ask, "Why do you play such violent games?" but never insisted we stop, although I recall there were some neighborhood boys who were not allowed to play with us when we played guns. I reckon that my constant asking after everyone, my vigilance, was sending the kids the same message my mom had sent me.

At one point, our stick ponies became the weapons. Honestly, the whole thing was really getting under my skin, but what made me intervene was the way they were waving those sticks around in one another's face. After several reminders about our rule against "swinging weapons," I intervened more firmly, saying, "I'm worried about those sticks. I keep seeing you guys poking them into each other's faces."

"But we're just shooting, Teacher Tom. They aren't swinging weapons."

"I understand, but it *looks* like you're swinging them in people's faces. It's my job to keep everyone safe. What you're doing doesn't look safe."

Henry looked at his stick pony weapon for a moment, then flipped it around so that the plush pony head end was forward. How about like this?"

"That part is soft and won't hurt as much if you accidentally hit someone in the face. Does everyone agree?"

Everyone agreed and the game recommenced.

Tom "Teacher Tom" Hobson is a preschool teacher, writer, speaker, artist, and author. He is best known, however, for his namesake blog, "Teacher Tom's Blog," where he has posted daily for over six years, chronicling the life and times of his little preschool in the rain-soaked Pacific Northwest corner of the United States. For the past fifteen years, Teacher Tom has been the sole employee of the Woodland Park Cooperative School, a collection of four separate parent-owned and -operated schools housed under a single roof, knit together by Teacher Tom's democratic, progressive play-based pedagogy. The children come to the school as two-year-olds in diapers and leave as "sophisticated" six-year-olds ready for the larger world.

LIONS LISTEN TO *NO!*

by Kelly Matthews

Inspired by a children's movie popular at the time, several children in my family child care program created a game they called "lions" that involved crawling on all fours, growling, and some pushing and shoving. The game forced me to revisit my thinking about rough-and-tumble play. I knew about the benefits of such play, but also felt aware of my responsibility to keep the younger children in my mixed-age setting safe.

As I saw this type of play ramping up, I decided to address it with the children to determine some frameworks for how this play could be done in a way that worked for everyone. My group was used to "making plans" about how we would spend our time together, and the children were accustomed to listening to each other and their planning, so I thought a planning session might be useful in thinking through the lions game.

Me: I noticed that you have been playing lots of "lions" lately. How do you play?

Sophie: You have to growl a lot.

Josh: Lions fight.

Me: What do the lions fight about?

Josh: Who is the strongest.

Me: How do they fight?

Sophie: They wrestle.

Me: Can we make a plan that you will only play this game with other lions who want to play?

[*Children agree.*]

ME: How will you know if someone wants to play?

SOPHIE: You can growl-ask them.

ME: What if they say no?

JOSH: Then you have to find another lion.

ME: I think that is a good plan. So, I have another question. How do you know when somebody doesn't want to play lions anymore?

SOPHIE: They could say *stop*!

ME: Do lions know how to understand English?

SOPHIE: For stop, they do.

ME: That's interesting, I thought they would only know Lion.

JOSH: They have to know "stop" because that is how we hafta be done.

ME: I think we can do that plan—"stop" means everyone freezes—then we can see if all the friends are okay. You can also watch the other lions' faces. How do lions look when they want to play?

SOPHIE: They could smile or laugh.

JOSH: They could say, "Growl-play-with-me-growl."

ME: What if they look scared? Or sad? Or really really mad? [*I make corresponding faces to match the emotions.*] Or what if they are crying? Is it okay to keep playing?

SOPHIE: Lions can ask, "Are you still playing?"

JOSH: Yeah, if they are crying you stop and get them a tissue!

[*We practice a few sessions of engaging as lions and I make sad or scared faces while wrestling. I ensure they have a working knowledge of what this would look like in play.*]

ME: Okay, before we play lions, can I tell you one more thing I am worried about with this game?

[*The children agree to listen.*] Sometimes we have little toddlers and babies here and they might not know you are pretending. I don't want them to think that you are fighting. They might be confused.

JOSH: You could keep the babies in the block room.

ME: I could, but what if they wanted to play with the other toys?

SOPHIE: You could tell the babies, "No no no, it's just pretend."

ME: I could, but babies and toddlers really do a lot of learning by watching other people.

JOSH, excitedly: What about Big Kid Friday? [*Due to a fluke in my scheduling, no toddlers or babies happened to attend on Fridays.*]

ME: What about it, Josh?

JOSH: We don't have babies come on Fridays. We could play lions all the time on Fridays!

ME: And not play it on the other days?

JOSH: Yeah!

ME: Sophie, do you agree with that plan?

Sophie smilingly growls a yes.

In addition to having this conversation, we practiced games such as Red Light, Green Light that supported impulse control. We played games that dealt with recognizing and showing emotion through facial expressions. I play wrestled with them and we practiced stopping on "Stop" or "No." I was pleased with the level of respect they showed each other when playing lions; they were careful to keep wrestling playful without bringing the playful aggression into real life. Occasionally the game intensity spiked and I heard the children ask each other, "Are you playing or are you done?" or state emphatically, "Lions listen to *no*!"

There were no injuries during this game and eventually the game wore off, but the deeper lessons about consent, understanding emotional displays, and how to be strong in their bodies stayed with these children.

Kelly Matthews, Harvest Resources Training Associate and owner of A Place for You Early Childhood Consulting in Oshkosh, Wisconsin, joyfully explores engaged learning with people of all ages. Over the past twenty years, she has worked in both center- and home-based care, as well as having been a director, nanny, mentor teacher, and professional development facilitator. Kelly earned her MA at Pacific Oaks College, with dual specializations in leadership in education and human services and early childhood education. Her passion is bringing relevant, thought-provoking professional development to educators and caregivers around the country.

CHAPTER FIVE

"This Feels Amazing"
Artistic Expression

"What does education do? It makes a straight-cut ditch out of a free, meandering brook."

—Henry David Thoreau,
from his journal (1850)

HOWARD CARTER SPENT DECADES WORKING as an archaeologist in Egypt, driven by the thought that each day might be *the* day, but by 1922, over thirty years after Carter arrived in Egypt, his funding was exhausted, and his time in the great desert neared its end. I imagine the heightened sense of urgency at the work site, an increased intensity during the team's long days of work, and a looming sense of fear that they would have to pack everything up and return to England with nothing of great significance to show for their decades of archaeological exploration. Then on November 4, 1922, just days before the dig was to end, he unearthed a stone step. Over the following weeks, the team carefully uncovered a staircase and a door that sat at the bottom. With great care, they entered and stood inside a magnificent room that had been sealed for centuries. The room branched off into hallways, leading one to another, and over the course of the following three months, every passageway was explored and every artifact was carefully documented, photographed, drawn, and eventually moved for analysis. The work was tedious. Three thousand years of burial made the artifacts extremely fragile, and extraordinary care was needed to slowly archive and remove the contents of the underground maze. Finally, on

February 16, 1923, the team reached the innermost chamber. Carefully opening up a tiny hole in the edge of the door, Carter inserted a light into the room to see. He found a burial chamber, filled with gold, decorated with funeral scenes, and, eventually, the sarcophagus of King Tutankhamun.

The work and methods of archaeologists during this period have been highly criticized, and while much of the criticism is warranted, the fact remains that these artifacts give researchers a unique glimpse into ancient Egyptian culture, opening a window to the Egyptians' beliefs, hopes, fears, values, and existential life crises. From these artifacts buried with the royalty of ancient Egypt, fragmented stone pillars standing impressively atop Machu Picchu, eighteenth-century Parisian textiles and furniture, and even through studying lists of films nominated for Academy Awards over the decades, anthropologists can hypothesize about the workings of a particular culture in its unique historical context. The creative products of civilizations provide windows into the questions at the heart of humanity. Art reflects and shapes what cultures view as valuable. In exploring the arts and culture of childhood, we can see the way that children understand beauty, art, and joy, and we gain a glimpse into pieces of their culture that would otherwise remain obscured.

Early Childhood Artifacts

I invite you to imagine what it would be like to be an archaeologist exploring an early childhood environment. Imagine if such an explorer were to open the door to an empty early childhood classroom or family child care room, moving about the sanitized spaces in search of cultural artifacts. What would she find? How would she categorize the arts and culture of this group? Would she see a calendar board noting the day's weather, graphing the number of children wearing red socks, and the days of the week? Would she find painted toilet paper tubes affixed with googly eyes and pipe cleaner hair hanging from the ceiling? Would she see a wall of nearly identical seasonal crafts displayed with each child's name in careful block lettering? Would she find seedlings at different phases of germination lining the windowsills and clinging to the windowpanes in foggy zipper storage bags? Would there be sand in a shallow table with dinosaurs buried alongside a three-wheeled truck and a plastic strainer? Where would she find the artifacts? Tacked with masking tape at child's-eye level or displayed with colorful backing at adult height? Would she find artifacts hidden in secret corners? A pile of cut paper clippings or a collection of leaf bits? When she pushes *play* on the music player, does she hear the sound of rolling ocean waves or a chorus of children singing and jumping or a folk singer picking on a guitar? What evidence exists that children inhabit the space? It is possible that in mining meaning from the cultural artifacts left behind by its childhood citizens, she might conclude that all children are driven by a desire for homogeneity, crafting rows of identical products. She might conclude that children enjoy visually bright and busy spaces, full of swinging and hanging things. She might conclude that children are a neat and orderly group of people. She might even conclude that children don't have much of a creative culture at all.

The challenge of exploring the arts and culture of children lies at the heart of childhood culture itself. Children are so thoroughly process oriented that products, in the typical sense, do not often remain as evidence of their exploration after the moment has passed. As is so often said of children, they would rather play with the box than the toy that came inside it. Children almost never see a paper bag and think to themselves, "Hey! I know! Let's stuff it and paint it orange, and then I will have the perfect seasonal craft!" And yet paper bag pumpkins and so many homogeneous products like them are the icons of early education. Surprisingly, after I moved to Switzerland from the United States and my son enrolled in a local child care program, he came home sporting many of the same products he would have created in product-oriented classrooms in the United States. Apparently, child care products are not bound by geography. And I wondered to myself, whose outcomes are these products attempting to measure?

Children whose artistic expressions are too governed by an end product often have difficulty nurturing a spirit of creativity and imagination that are foundational to the learning process. The question is, do such product-oriented creations reflect the true culture of childhood, particularly the creative processes of children? And if not, why does uniformity still have such a stronghold in early childhood settings?

The Process Is the Art

One afternoon in my family child care program, I had the great opportunity to observe a child's process-oriented nature at work. I watched two-year-old Simone working with a chubby wooden-handled brush and a chalky splotch of tempera at the bottom of an aluminum cake pan. What started off as a reasonable squirt of a single color whose destiny was to mingle with the brush and end up on a piece of paper was transformed into an altogether different product. She stared transfixed into the cake pan as if discovering the meaning of the universe. Methodically and slowly, she swirled the brush around the perimeter of the pan. Then she moved the brush purposefully from the pan to her bare arm. She rotated her arm at the elbow, and deftly covered her skin from midarm to wrist, with slow, somber intention. Once her arm canvas was saturated, she moved to her hand, and I watched with joy as she began to paint her palm.

As she worked, she floated on a different plane, exploring with the care and intrigue of an astronaut landing on an unexplored planet for the first time. Moving from her palm to the back of her hands and on to her fingertips, I saw her mouth the words *this feels amazing* in slow, methodic repetition, a mantra reflecting the deep meditative experience she was having. I sat at the same table and watched, but she was entirely unconscious of my presence.

I still get chills when I remember this experience. I was an outsider witnessing a ceremonial rite of sorts: a child fully immersed in the present moment, absorbed entirely within her senses. After soap and water, no product remained to testify to the magnitude of the experience.

There was no painting, at least in the traditional "brush and paper" sense, no tangible product to send home to an eager parent. Only experience floated in the room that day. Simone was two, and an emotional memory of the experience probably dissipated after the soap bubbles made their way down the drain. But the experience, and so many others like it, was hardwired into the core of her brain, undergirding her thoughts and reactions in the years to come. The lack of an end product does nothing to diminish the significance of the experience, and this is the heart of the arts and culture of childhood.

For the artists in early childhood environments, the process *is* the art. The end product is not even a blip in their universe. Yet, as adults, we face extreme barriers to really understanding the value of a process-oriented approach. Scores of books exist on the importance of process-oriented learning, filled with pages of ideas to help educators embrace a more open-ended program. In the arena of early childhood professional development, there has been an upswing of classes about emergent learning and project-based approaches, all motivated by the idea that children need to discover and explore without a clearly defined end point. I can't remember the last time I attended a conference and heard a speaker defend teacher-directed, cookie-cutter-type projects as best practice (projects that would have teachers directing students to "cut on these lines," "glue these shapes in this order," or "color this part green").

Still, our conferences and professional literature sit a comfortable distance from actual practice, and I know it is hard for teachers to abandon what they have been doing for years. We can emotionally enjoy the experience of watching children who are living fully in the moment, and we can appreciate the value of letting children explore with the various materials in their environment, but at the same time, we continue to hold a strong attachment to the things children produce. After all, how would the day begin in our early childhood settings if not for thirty minutes of circle time focused on the calendar where we produce evidence of our work in the form of added dates and icons about the weather? What would the toddler room look like if not for the seasonal crafts of paper bag pumpkins and egg carton caterpillars? What would the parents of infants do without the butterflies made out of their precious children's footprints? Change is difficult, so even if we believe professionally and intellectually in the ideas of process-oriented approaches, we have grown to expect certain products at certain ages. Ultimately, however, it isn't our sentimental connection to the products that makes change the most difficult; we desperately lack any transformative language to validate and support a wholly new approach.

The Child's Relationship with Time

The heart of this dilemma lies in an unexpected tension between the culture of adults and the culture of children in our divergent understandings of time. For adults, time is a commodity to be spent, earned, made, invested, saved, and used wisely, and the only way we know to accurately assess the value of our "investment" is in the product of our time. Think about the various ways we talk about our days: "I wasted three hours on Facebook," or "I was so productive . . . I read two chapters, organized my filing cabinet, and called Joey's father about chaperoning our field trip," or "I sat in traffic for forty-five minutes on the way to my meeting," or "I had to wait for two hours in the emergency room." We run a perpetual time deficit, blaming our lack of time for our insufficient self-care while we multitask constantly. In fact, if I find myself in a waiting room with nothing productive to read and no headphones in my pocket to continue my audio books, I feel a tinge of panic. We have outgrown our ability to move from one thought to the next without a measurable end point. In part, this is a critical and necessary shift from childhood to adulthood. Imagine an example of adults employing a process-oriented approach to a task in their daily lives. If every walk from one place to the next were full of the wondering curiosity of a toddler, we would never get anywhere.

Our cultural construction of time shapes our working lives. Because we understand time as a measure of value, then the products we create with time are evidence of how effectively we used it. As early childhood professionals, many of our salaries are paid in units of time; our rates are often calculated by the hour, day, week, or month. Therefore, our productivity is measured by those same units of time. The culture of childhood, however, does not conceive of time in economic terms, and therefore resists the pressure of time as a motivating factor in children's work. Bringing this bias to weigh on their creative process imposes a pressure that does not exist within their cultural framework.

Since our worth as human beings is consistently defined by what we produce, anything devoid of production is essentially worthless. Early childhood professionals are bound in a difficult way to conflicting interpretations of time. We work with a population who doesn't share our concern for products nor our attachment to the future, and yet these are the rubrics by which we (and our stakeholders: parents, fellow colleagues, administrators, and the surrounding community) measure our effectiveness. Even if we buy into the idea of a process-oriented approach, without products, how will we validate the work we do? One of the children in my family child care program hated to be involved in art *anything*. He was repelled by paint, glue, markers, crayons, stickers, playdough, or other typically magnetic materials for young children, preferring instead to immerse himself in the book corner. Occasionally, he would be drawn by the invitation to cut paper into little pieces, but besides a pile of homemade confetti, I rarely had products to offer his mother. She watched while the other children gushed over their creations, a tinge of desire eclipsing her happiness at the fact that her son spent his days following his passions. I reassured his mother: he will paint when he wants to paint, draw when he wants to draw, and by honoring his passions now in the present, he will be able to closely articulate his passions in the future. Also, by forcing a task on him, he is less likely to enjoy it or connect with it, so any cognitive benefits are diluted with reluctance.

For children, strict adherence to a clock interferes with their ability to engage deeply and creatively. So say Elizabeth Jones and Gretchen Reynolds in *The Play's the Thing*:

Time, it is clear, can be managed in many ways. Some ways are responsive to young children's erratic pace and to the wide variation in pace among individuals, supporting autonomy and enabling children to exert initiative in largely uninterrupted play. Other ways are clock-controlled and group-focused, attempting to move all the children together. In such programs children get practice for the constraints they may later find in public school, but restricted opportunity to practice the initiative that is the developmental challenge for competent 3- to 5-year olds. (2011, 30)

Our connections to a clock are cultural; we can choose to structure a different experience for our young ones that is based more on their cultural perception of time and its value.

Children are process oriented, but they still create. In exploring the nature of their creative expression, we find evidence of depth of process-oriented learning. Just as the relics left in King Tutankhamun's tomb paint a picture of life in ancient Egypt, pieces of the young child's life reveal the nature of their culture as a process-oriented community.

As an early childhood educator, I sometimes find myself trolling Pinterest boards of art activities, dreaming about the projects I could make with my young companions. Invariably, I decide—against my better judgment—to try a project that is just too intriguing for me to pass up. One of my more memorable failures was attempting to make a multicolored collection of yarn ornaments to hang along a string of tiny white lights. The project was wonderful, and the result would be whimsical, if we could only make it to the finished product. I knew my young ones would agree that it was worth the effort. The project involved inflating small balloons to the size of a tennis ball, and then covering them with string that had been soaked in white glue. Sounds like fun! Then, after the glue dried, you were supposed to be able to pop the balloons and pull out the pieces to reveal a really cool lacy skeleton that you could then hang around tiny (heatless LED) lights.

We sat down with the necessary supplies and I explained the idea to my group, but I failed to account for one variable in the plan. The group was eager to start, but once they saw the balloons, they became far too compelled to move on to the string and glue. They started bouncing the balloons across the table to one another, and running to launch them from the highest points in the room. I worked hard, with no success, to bring them back to the table so they could get to work doing a "really cool project." I sat for a few minutes working with the string and glue, thinking that if I just got it started, they might think it was intriguing enough to join me. But as they ran and jumped and squealed with delight, I was reminded of my deep commitment to a process-oriented approach, knowing that a spark of curiosity should be followed to its natural end.

As the children played, they asked to bring out our shop vac (a small, industrial vacuum cleaner only ever used for play). We attached the hose to "blow" and explored with the high-powered air for the rest of the morning. After a time, I brought out baskets of cotton balls and feathers to add to their exploration, and some time later, we changed the vacuum hose to "suck" mode to gather all the cotton balls and feathers into the tank again for later use. When the children left for the day, I sat down again with a bowl of glue, some string, and a balloon, too eager for a cool set of lights to resist crafting myself. After thirty minutes of trying to keep the string stuck to the balloon, I gave up, grateful that I had not tried to force this project on the group.

Child-Centered Creativity

To fully understand the arts and culture of children, let's look at the types of creating that children do when they are left to follow their own ends without any oversight from adults. True childhood arts and culture are not driven to a finished product. Instead, the arts and culture of children are driven by three distinct elements.

Urgent Need

The first drive to create is urgent need. Sometimes in the course of play, children discover a gap in available materials, and that gap prompts the creation of play props, like hats for pirates, cell phones for busy parents, or bus tickets for an impromptu imaginary field trip. Once, the children in my group were involved in a game of kings and queens. One of the children chose her favorite whimsical fabric and wrapped it around her waist like a skirt. She began looking for the wand only to discover that it was in use. This lack created a sense of panic among the players. How would they play kings and queens if there were no available wands? One child suggested that kings and queens don't need wands. Another suggested that the kings and queens share power over a single wand. Neither idea gained traction. Finally, as the group of players huddled around the problem, someone suggested *making* new wands. The whole group eagerly and wholeheartedly agreed.

There was an element of urgency in their voices as if this project were a departure from the play they were sculpting. All the children worked with an intense focus, setting their sights on the goal of a sufficient number of props to support the play. They gathered all the odd bits they could find and worked furiously to create magnificent and powerful wands.

Sometimes, these artifacts are discarded when their usefulness has expired, repurposed in a new pursuit, or abandoned in a basket of props. In the case of the wands, the children continued to use them for a few days, but only in the kings and queens script. No single child showed an interest in taking the wand home or displaying it in any capacity other than as a support for play.

Curious Exploration

A second drive to create resides in a curiosity about the materials themselves. The flexibility inherent in the children's process-oriented approach is the cornerstone of their culture. Too rigid a vision, and children grow frustrated at their lack of skills to execute the plan. The flexibility of an open-ended plan encourages their creative minds to move fluidly from one moment to the next, as in the following story of a child making birds.

A jar of googly eyes and pom-pom balls was sufficiently compelling for a bird-loving child in my program to begin fashioning her own collection of feathered friends. At the outset, she knew she wanted to make birds, but the execution and final project were undefined. She encountered challenges—pom-pom balls that would not stay stuck together or eyes sliding to the wrong end of the head—and her design changed. More materials accommodated the shifting plans, and her script kept changing to make room for this unwieldy puffy creature. In the beginning, she wanted a baby bird, but as the body size kept growing, the bird took on new characteristics: first it transformed into an older sibling, then into a mommy, and finally it became a daddy. Once she solved the puzzle of creating the birds, she duplicated her process several times to make a whole family, which then needed a nest, which then needed a basket to carry the nest, and finally a bird costume for the child so she could properly parent her flock.

Anyone who has spent any time with children knows that specialty art items like googly eyes, colorful feathers, sequins, gold or silver pipe cleaners, and glitter glue hold a special magnetism for young children and often spark this kind of intense curiosity and exploration. I always purchased such items with some reticence, because they tended to be comparatively expensive and purchasing the specialty items left me with less of a budget to spend on other art materials. I would dispense these treasures carefully, ensuring equity and frugality. Once, I took the plunge and purchased a giant jar of a thousand googly eyes, thinking they would last for a long time. The jar was discovered by two three-year-olds while I was busy in another area, and they could not contain their excitement. So I brought out the jar and poured a reasonably generous amount (twenty?) into a bowl for the two girls to use. What they asked for next surprised me. They wanted balloons. *Balloons?* Yes. Balloons. One child would stretch the neck of a balloon, and the other child would painstakingly insert the googly eyes into the hole, working them slowly down until they fell into the cavity. They worked with unwavering concentration, continuing to ask for more materials. I was filled with curiosity, but also some resistance—was this the reason I purchased those expensive little eyes? To fill balloons? My curiosity won out, and I kept their bowl of eyes filled as needed until they had used the better part of that new jar and two bags of balloons.

Stuffing balloons with googly eyes was an odd choice for a morning of exploration, to be sure, but an experience that they pursued from after breakfast, across morning snacktime, and right up until lunch. Periodically, I was called over to inflate one of the eye-stuffed balloons. As the air inflated the cavity, eyes swirled like a tornado, hushing against the stretching material. Filled and tied, the balloons became immediate musical instruments, with the eyes making a loud noise as they bounced around in the balloon. In the afternoon, the two girls organized a group of toddlers to accompany them in a marching band of chanting percussionists, repeating in unison the chorus: "We are the lions. We are the lions." Several days later, the balloons were abandoned and starting to pucker and deflate. I gathered them one afternoon, cut the ends off, and refilled the jar of eyes, pleased that they could be repurposed before they were used up for good.

The curiosity-driven arts and culture of young children might not actually produce any identifiable "art" to match the investment of time, energy, and resources that adults might expect. The lack of an expected product can conflict not only with our perceptions of how time is valued but also with how we think resources are managed. Children—by adult standards—are wasteful. Left unmonitored, a group of curious toddlers could run through a whole package of glitter glue in ten minutes. Children paint until the weight tears holes in their paper. If left to secure their own materials, they will use whole bottles of glue in one sitting. The youngest in my program would use entire sheets of stickers at once, sometimes adhering the stickers one on top of the other to create a pile in the middle of a piece of paper. Older children and returning kindergartners, on the other hand, would be more judicious in their sticker usage, saving their favorites for a prominent spot on their shirts. I always engaged in an internal debate about the purpose of art materials in my early childhood program. Did I have some responsibility to teach the children about conservation and the dangers of wasteful usage? Or was my job to simply sit back and let children create what they saw fit?

Children use resources as a way of facilitating their quest for understanding. We know that the *intended* purpose of glue is to stick one object to another, but children might wonder what would happen if it were poured in a pile or drizzled from a craft stick or rubbed on their bodies. We know that the *intended* purpose of sequins is to decorate projects, but children might wonder what sequins would look like in a pile or shaken in a balloon or thrown around the room. (Later in this chapter, we will look at the child's perception of cleaning up.) Once, I observed a child using two sequins as a pair of glasses through which to assess her progress. Her paper was filled with various shapes and sizes of neatly organized sequins that were not glued in place, but merely waiting for a turn to be tested as lenses. She put down one pair and picked up the next, holding them in front of her squinting eyes in order to look at her work in new ways. We must try to keep our knowledge of the intended purposes of materials in check, because defining the purpose of a material moves it from a place of process-oriented learning to a closed, fixed product.

At the same time, we still face the issue of cost and waste that accompanies a young child's culture. As an adult, I understand that the unwanted castoffs will end up in a landfill and that replacing art materials is a costly endeavor. And yet, through the child's lens, the materials reveal the magic of the world. My daughter was born with limitless curiosity, and when she was three, I used to find glue sticks, rolled all the way up and broken off—the rolls of glue laying on pieces of construction paper under her bed. I asked about them, and she would tell me, matter-of-factly: "I'm making an experiment." I stopped her experiments, reasoning that glue is for sticking things together and expressing my desire not to have the glue wasted. Even as I said these things to her, I realized the conflict between my adult ways of perceiving the world and her child-oriented perception, but I felt I needed to make a case for keeping the glue sticks for their intended purpose. In her mind, the glue was serving its exact purpose—to tell her what would happen if it were left exposed to the air. As the rolled glue dried, she found she could massage it into little balls of gummy—though no longer sticky—material. Transformed before her eyes, this process was like magic, and it was a process she was not eager to abandon. The experience she designed was an authentic, child-led inquiry, building a foundation for a passion for learning. Later, she would pour rivers of glue onto pieces of cardboard or construction paper and let them sit so she could test what would happen. Once I found a plastic spoon that had been filled with glue just so she could observe. She would break the tips of markers to mix the ink into puddles of glue. She would cut crayons with scissors, dissect an entire ball of yarn into one-inch segments, make giant tape balls with masking tape to see if they would stick when they hit the wall. In short, she did not naturally make conservative use of materials.

In the end, I came to the conclusion that she was in charge of the materials. I was responsible for purchasing what was within my budget, and she was responsible for how it was used. If all the glue ran out before my budget or time allowed for more, then she would have to think creatively about how to solve problems that are typically solved with glue. The same was true for the markers, crayons, paint, and so on. This was a practice I extended to my family child care program, because my daughter's story is the rule, not the exception. Children are driven to experiment, and the materials they have serve their unending curiosities. Many children may not say, "I'm making an experiment," but that is exactly what drives their inquiry. This is what is going on when toddlers color the same spot of a piece of paper over and over until the paper tears. This is what is happening when infants smear food on their trays or five-year-olds paint with their hands. They are discovering the world, and we must make space for that.

Along with my commitment to keeping materials accessible, I also stocked my supply cabinets with recycled materials. I put the word out to family, friends, and clients that I needed their empty cereal and cracker boxes, paper that had print only on one side, half-used balls of yarn, plastic caps from water bottles, and on and on. My budget went largely toward glue, tape, paint, and markers. I abandoned the idea of specialty materials (with rare exceptions), and stuck to things that could be replaced inexpensively or repurposed for another project down the line.

Relational Art

A third element of children's drive to create concerns what I call "relational art." Relational art is born out of the child's emotional connection to other people, as in this story of two-year-old Minh, who spent the morning working on a project for her mother. As she worked, she chanted a single phrase over and over, "My mama is going to *love* this!" With every sticker, each fringe cut out of the edge of the repurposed cereal box, and all the letters sketched on the back (a whole alphabet of invented spelling on the reverse side), her excitement grew. *"My mama is going to* love *this!"* Minh beamed as she finished her creation. When it was done, she placed it in her cubby and waited for the moment when she could give it to her mother. Minh visited her artwork periodically throughout the day, too eager to leave it resting unadmired, and she would occasionally add an embellishment here or there that she found lacking in the form of a stray googly eye or a piece of cut yarn. With so much attention throughout the day, her artwork lost some of its extras, but it was with a heart bursting with love that Minh presented it at the end of the day to her mama, who received the gift in the spirit in which it was intended—matching love for love—and thus offering back to her daughter what was most desired.

Children do create artistic works, but their concept of time keeps them so rooted in the present that the products of their efforts are sometimes relatively unimportant in their minds. In addition to the props eventually discarded, and the symbols of curiosity like glue puddles abandoned to dry, there remains one type of product children create that is intensely important and valuable—the products created for loved ones. Products children create for their friends and family members are most meaningful when they are designed and executed from within the imagination of the child. A teacher-directed craft is still a work of love, but the child—who has not wrestled this product out of his own imagination—is distanced from it.

Beyond the Art Table: Process-Oriented Lives

For children, the process-oriented framework affects more than just their artistic expression, and as we look beyond the paper, markers, paints, and glue at the art table, we find further evidence of the cultural pattern of a process-oriented approach. In an article in the *Harvard Educational Review*, Vivian Gussin Paley recounted insights during her early years as a teacher. She told of a particular *a-ha* moment that occurred while she was observing a novice teacher, Bill, who was working with Paley's class:

> He asked a question or made a casual observation, then repeated each child's comment and hung onto it until a link was made to someone else's idea. Together they were constructing a paper chain of magical imaginings mixed with some solid facts, and Bill was providing the glue. . . . He had few expectations of what five-year-olds might say or think, and he listened to their responses with the anticipation one brings to the theater when a mystery is being revealed. Bill was interested not in what he knew to be an answer, but only in how the children intuitively approached a problem. . . . I began to copy Bill's style whenever the children and I had formal discussions. I practiced his open-ended questions, *the kind that seek no specific answers but rather build a chain of ideas without the need for closure.* (1986, 123; italics mine)

When I read this passage, I had an *a-ha* moment of my own. Engaging with children without a script and without a predetermined point of closure is at the heart of a process-oriented disposition. Children carry this disposition into the classroom, not just for their creative processes but for the whole of classroom life as well. I started to think of all the types of conversations we have with children and how much of those conversations is driven by "right" and "wrong" answers. The songs we sing have "right" and "wrong" sounds and motions—the horn on the bus goes *beep-beep*, the cow on the farm says *moo*, and five little monkeys jump on the bed before four. As we read books, we ask questions that have right and wrong answers—identifying the color of the ball, the location of the bird, or finding baby's bellybutton. The content of our everyday dialogue is filled with right and wrongs: calendar time in the mornings, counting lessons, and even simple conversations about what the child ate for breakfast. Some of our management techniques are embedded in a style of questioning that supposedly leads children to an understanding of right and wrong: "Where do the shoes go?" "What should your feet be doing in the classroom?" "Who hit first?" To be truly process oriented would require an unscripted approach to the classroom that might throw us all for a loop!

The process-oriented disposition of childhood is at odds with the product-oriented nature of adulthood. Evidence of the cultural conflict infuses everything we do; it's not limited to a child's creative work. Studying the culture of childhood reveals aspects of children's broader experience outside the "Creation Station" or "Art Nook." As their lives spill over into their full days, they bring this process-oriented lens to everything they do.

Cleanup Time

Just last night as I was asking my children to pick up their bedrooms before bedtime (you couldn't walk from the door to the bed without tripping), my daughter responded, "Why do we need to clean up? We'll just have to get it out all over again." She has a valid point, and it's a question I've come back to repeatedly in my work with young children. Cleaning up is a process that, on its face, is at odds with the important work children do. They work for hours to build a fort only to tear it down. They are pulled fiercely into a play script of grocery store or dragons, and while they are at the peak of the story line, the lunch bell signals that it's time to clean it up.

I found an e-card floating around on Facebook once that said, "Cleaning with kids in the house is like eating Oreos while brushing your teeth." While I laughed at the sentiments of this card, I also sensed a certain one-sidedness in the conversation. I suspect that much of the respect for children and the sense of communal ownership over the space has been removed from the process. In the days of cluttered floors, disordered bookcases, and emptied Tupperware drawers, I am exhausted from repeatedly caring for a space in which my co-inhabitors have a different idea of how to keep the space than I do.

Cleanup is difficult for children for a few reasons. First, as was discussed in chapter 3, constant interruptions and reminders to clean up are disrespectful of the child's process. When I am in the middle of a project, and I must leave that project to run an errand or prepare a meal, I have ways to save the process by adding bookmarks to my books or closing my computer. I don't reshelf books that I am in the middle of reading, nor do I pack my computer away if I am planning to come back. Interruptions are still disorienting, but perhaps we can find ways to help children save their play across different times of the day. Second, imposing my idea of order on children's construct of what-goes-where leaves them voiceless regarding their space. Children should have a say in where they find their things. Third, expecting young children to manage the entire cleanup process independently is developmentally inappropriate. For young children who are still working on skills of categorizing and working memory, the task of sorting out and relocating an entire day's worth of play is simply too much to ask.

So why clean up at all? Again, I think there are several reasons why the practice of cleaning up together is still important in early childhood classrooms. When children know where to find things, they are free to explore and create without the anxiety of having to search for materials. Order helps encourage respect for materials. If the dress-up clothes are stored in a pile in the corner, children are less likely to care for them because they aren't even worthy of a designated spot in the room. Cleaning up is important for safety. More than once, I have stepped barefoot on a stegosaurus or a block, and it is not an experience I'm hoping to repeat. Finally, the process of cleaning up is as much for my sanity as the children's, and this makes it a high priority. Respect is about everyone's needs being met, and if I ignore my need for order for the sake of allowing the children to pursue their wildest dreams, I am still operating disrespectfully and compromising self-care.

Allowing the culture of childhood to inform our practice means shifting our ideas about cleanup time. We have to abandon our traditionally manipulative methods of orchestrating a cleanup effort, including competitions ("Who can be the fastest one to clean up the blocks?"), asking questions I already know the answer to as a way of getting children to clean up ("Do you know where the dolls go?"), using praise ("Look at what a good block cleaner Simone is. I wish everyone could clean blocks like Simone!"), or threats ("No lunch until you finish your job with the blocks!"). Instead, let's consider these ideas:

Move past "us" and "them." I clean up *with* the children. If I want them to help me, I model by helping them. Replace "I didn't make the mess so I shouldn't clean it up!" with "You look like you could use a hand. Can I help?"

Respect the fact that children are using the space and materials. I wouldn't want someone cleaning up my projects without first asking my permission; therefore I do not clean up materials children have used until I first ask if they are done. "Raquel? I noticed the blocks are out. Are you still playing with them? Do you mind if I put them away?"

Use direct and clear, manipulation-free communication. If I say, "Raquel, the blocks are still out. Are you still playing with them?" as a way of passively getting her to clean them up, then I am not being clear. I can say, "Raquel? I noticed the blocks are still out, and you look like you're done playing with them. You need to put them away. Would you like help?"

Be flexible when possible. Not everything needs to get put away in exactly the right place every day. Not everything needs to get put away at the moment its usefulness has passed. Not everything needs to be put away cheerfully and with a smile. Transitions are hard, especially ones that signal the end of play.

Foster a sense of community responsibility. Children should not have to keep track of each item they played with and be responsible for its relocation. Instead of "I didn't play with the blocks, so I don't have to help clean them up," empower children with choice over their environment: "Tell me what you see that you can put away." A powerful sense of community forms when children share ownership of the entire space rather than trying to just manage the messes they made.

Living with Cultural Differences

So how do we manage the confluence of adult and childhood cultures? What is to be done in a world of adults who seek measurable outcomes and identifiable products as evidence of effectiveness? In part, we must look for products in different places—the inhomogeneity of a bucket of loose parts, the odd bits of yarn and ribbon gathered together with glue, or the evolving story lines hovering like fog in the classroom landscape. We have to train ourselves to align our expectations with what is culturally meaningful for children, bound with them to the present in the way that we are bound to the future. Our awareness of the child's work communicates that what she is doing is worthy of attention. The time we take to write a note about her clever story, the significance we place on her effort when we sit to draw a model of her block fort, when we photograph her costumes, make audio recordings of her invented songs, retell stories of her ingenuity and creativity to her family—in each of these instances, we are communicating that the processes she engages in are significant.

We must be aware, however, of the reasons why we make these records. We can document the work of children as a way of respectfully affirming the value of what they do every day and to learn from their process, or these records can stand as proof of children's limited voices in early childhood settings. All the photographing, writing anecdotes, connecting observable moments to written standards can impose a culture on children that is not their own, and be acts of cultural appropriation whereby we use the work of childhood to serve the demands of adulthood. If childhood continues to be held captive to the demands of the culture of adulthood, children remain powerless over how their actions are interpreted and used, and they remain voiceless.

The purpose of early childhood education is not strictly to document all the deposits into a child's future. It is not solely an accounting of the valuable endeavors of each day. Children have a right to explore, experiment, wonder, and create, even if those explorations cannot be immediately linked to measurable goals and objectives. Documenting a child's learning is important. Articulating the profound experiences that take place from day to day is important. Reflecting on children's daily routines in our programs is important. But sometimes we can't name all the mathematical, linguistic, and social payoffs from a morning of rich, process-oriented exploration. Perhaps, at some point, the fact that our children do the best job they can do at being children is simply enough.

Stories from the Field

"IT'S A ZOO!"

by Kelly Matthews

Children in my multiage family child care program had large chunks of time to develop their play and play scripts, and had fairly free use of materials. Items from one area might fill a need in another; dramatic play props, for example, might end up in the book area or the block area or the art area. We'd clean up when necessary and children would help put things back so they could be found again.

The play worlds children create are powerful and I believe fully that children deserve the power of determination in those worlds—defining what and how those worlds work, posing theories, and determining outcomes. Children often verbally described these ideas, definitions, and details of play, but sometimes they needed print and signage to clarify and communicate those details in other ways. Children are competent in processing the world around them and notice the details of communication and use them in ways to further their play.

Lexi brought magnetic blocks (building materials with embedded magnets) to a table, along with some animals, and began creating an enclosure for her animals. She started with a floor, and then began on the walls. She thoughtfully sized the enclosure to fit the animals she wanted to include, intentionally picked building shapes that contributed to symmetry, and finished with equilateral triangles on the top edges of the wall for some flair in her design.

When completed, she wanted her friends to know clearly what she had created. It wasn't a barn or a castle and it surely wasn't a house. She was aware that locations often have signage declaring names of places or functions of space. She went to the art center and got a piece of paper and a brown marker and carefully lettered out *Z-O*. I had been casually watching her work as I was playing with other children—she caught my eye and asked: "Is there a silent one?" (We had been talking about silent *e*'s in words.) I told her, "Not exactly—for this word, two letters work together to make that *oo* sound." She looked up from her paper. "Another *o*?" she ventured. I nodded my head and she completed the second *o*. She grabbed a pair of scissors and carefully cut around her word. She clipped off several pieces of tape and walked back to her structure. She affixed the sign to her building without pausing to ask if it was okay to tape on toys (I was happy to see that she knew what she was doing would be supported). Lexi was accustomed to an environment that explored the power of print. She paused in her play to use that knowledge to define her play world. She understood the multiple functions of print and she harnessed that power to make her play more nuanced.

———————————————

Kelly Matthews, Harvest Resources Associate and owner of A Place for You Early Childhood Consulting in Oshkosh, Wisconsin, joyfully explores engaged learning with people of all ages. Over the past twenty years, she has worked in both center- and home-based care, as well as having been a director, nanny, mentor teacher, and professional development facilitator. Kelly earned her MA at Pacific Oaks College, with dual specializations in leadership in education and human services and early childhood education. Her passion is bringing relevant, thought-provoking professional development to educators and caregivers around the country.

CHAPTER SIX

"Look at Me!"
The Economics of Belonging

"Earlier is not better. All children accomplish milestones in their own way in their own time."

—Magda Gerber

"When I grow up, I'll probably be an opera, because when the music is on, I sing and sing and sing. You can probably hear me because I'm kind of shouting because it's beautiful and I want people to hear."

—Simone, age four

SYSTEMS OF ECONOMICS HAVE PROFOUND and far-reaching influence. In the economy of adulthood, themes of scarcity, competition, and getting what is deserved govern the ways we think about value and worth. Importantly, these beliefs about worth and value shape far more than monetary transactions. Strings are always attached, even in relationships, as evidenced by the unspoken accounting of who pays for dinner, the list of people you can call to help you move, and reciprocity in gift exchanges. Most significantly for our work, this system of economics profoundly shapes our interactions with young children, particularly in regards to managing their behavior.

Our economic mind-set created a ripe environment for the behaviorist model of raising children, made popular in the 1890s by a psychologist named Ivan Pavlov and his now famous dog. In a series of experiments, Pavlov systematically conditioned his dog to salivate merely at the sound of a bell.

Behaviorism grew over the subsequent decades, and in the 1920s, a scientist named John Watson extended this understanding of systematic conditioning to the world of young children. Watson's "Little Albert Experiment" as it has come to be known, involved giving an eleven-month-old boy, Albert, a soft white rat to play with, and then scaring Albert by jumping out from behind and yelling in a loud, frightening voice. The experiment was repeated: Albert played with the rat and Watson scared him. It didn't take long to change Albert's response to the rat from curiosity, wonder, and joy into terror. He cowered at the sight of the rat because he associated it with fear. Watson believed that the power of adults to mold their young children was an incredibly strong force. His words, penned nearly a century ago, echo in our practices with young children today: "Give me a dozen healthy infants, well-formed, and my own specified world to bring them up in, and I'll guarantee to take any one at random and train him to become any type of specialist I might select—doctor, lawyer, artist—regardless of his talents, penchants, tendencies, abilities, vocations, and race of his ancestors" (quoted in Plucker 2007). Watson believed adult behavior would be the deciding factor in a child's outcome.

In practice today, behaviorism looks like this: a child who misbehaves is punished; a child who behaves is rewarded; a child who is annoying is ignored. We condition our children, through our responses, to "behave correctly." Nothing in life is free, not even in the context of child–adult relationships. Children must earn everything because that is *just the way things are,* from tangible things such as allowances or special gifts to attention from parents to time for relaxation and entertainment. Our adult economic framework creates a model whereby everything in life must be earned, even in our most important relationships. Writer Alfie Kohn says, "The laws of the marketplace—supply and demand, tit for tat—have assumed the status of universal and absolute principles, as though everything in our lives, including what we do with our children, is analogous to buying a car or renting an apartment. . . . After all, people shouldn't get something for nothing. Not even happiness. Or love" (2005, 17–18). In the context of economics, relationships are driven by conditions, and to be worthy of a relationship is not a guarantee.

Out of this economic narrative spring many of our misconstrued ideas about the culture of childhood. For example, picking up a crying infant is "spoiling" her and "teaching her to cry for attention." Attending to a toddler who is having a tantrum is "letting yourself be manipulated." Four-year-olds who are not adequately punished for their misdeeds are "getting away with it." The problem is that children do not live with the same narrative. The economics of childhood culture look radically different from that of the culture of adulthood. We apply our own adult economic biases to children at great cost to their developing sense of belonging. Actress and comedian Lily Tomlin once joked, "The trouble with being in the rat race is that even if you win, you're still a rat." What if children aren't running the same race we're running? What if they aren't even racing, but instead are working together to build a blanket fort?

Economics in the Culture of Childhood: The Need to Belong

In exploring the economics of childhood the way an anthropologist would, we aren't going to find capitalism or free markets or a formal system managing the exchange and production of goods and services. What we will find are unique perceptions of wealth, value, and scarcity. The economics of childhood are a system of values rooted in belonging. Children measure the value of objects, people, and experiences in relational terms: Do I belong to my community? Am I a valued participant? Am I influential and powerful? What currency do I have that makes me influential? In the same way that adults can judge their economic value by totaling their currency, children use a kind of relational currency to assess the extent of their belonging. For children, that currency is a combination of attention and connection. They know how much they matter by the extent to which they feel connected and attended to by those they love.

The culture of childhood clearly does not operate with the same economic narratives that drive the culture of adulthood. The child's mechanism for finding value and meaning in the world looks radically different from the economic structure of adulthood. Children do not operate with strings attached, nor do they naturally thrive in competitive environments (though we often start them on such a heavy dose of competition at such a young age that they grow to accept it as a way of life). Children do have a concept of investment and they do relate to the idea of scarcity, but the ways in which they invest and the model they use for understanding scarcity are entirely different from the model of adulthood.

When we understand that children approach the world through a lens of belonging, we can appreciate aspects of the young child's day with new insight. The difficulty children face at separating from loved ones represents a threat to their sense of belonging. Attention-seeking behavior is a sign that children don't feel as if they belong or that they feel their connection is tenuous. Children's desires for particular toys or experiences often represent a longing to be relevant and contributing members of a peer community. At the heart of the economic system of childhood lie two questions: "How do I find belonging with my peers?" and "Do I still belong to my family community while I am away?"

The Danger of Running Too Fast

One sunny afternoon as I returned home with the children in my family child care program, I watched the interaction between two-year-old Esther and four-year-old Bryan. The two were running happily along the path, laughing as they went. Esther moved more slowly than Bryan, more shakily on her legs than he did, but the game persisted despite their athletic differences. As I watched more closely, I noticed something compelling. Bryan would run a little way ahead and then turn around, eyebrows raised, and smile directly at Esther. He would chant in a singsongy kind of voice, "You can't catch me!" He mimicked the kind of play I'm sure he'd engaged in with his family many times, regulating his running speed so that Esther could keep up.

The game was not a speed challenge; there was clearly no race that either child sought to win. They ran together as a form of play and friendship, sharing a common experience. Later, I walked with Bryan, and I said to him, "Bryan, you and Esther were really having fun together."

"Yes. She likes to run with me."

"I could tell. She looked very happy."

Then Bryan said something profound, revealing a great insight into his understanding of belonging. "I knew I had to run slow. If I ran fast, she wouldn't be able to play, and she would leave the game." He knew belonging depended on his ability to regulate his speed. There was a danger in running too fast: Esther might become disinterested, or she might get angry and cry. In any event, the likely result of Bryan's running too fast would be a stop to the game. He was motivated to slow down because of empathy; he knew Esther would want to play and responded in a very compassionate way. And he was also motivated by a strong and intuitive sense of belonging; the culture of childhood works more smoothly when children have a place to belong. The economics of adulthood are steeped in competition, but the culture of childhood stands in belonging. Sure, children want to be the fastest, run the farthest, and push their abilities to the limits, but just as often, we see signs of children who use their abilities in creative ways to find belonging with peers.

Children find belonging through more than just comparing their abilities. Other elements of childhood—possessions, knowledge, and experiences—are what give children belonging. Sociologist Allison Pugh writes about consumer culture and childhood, and she makes the powerful observation that "having 'nothing to say' is akin to not belonging, to a sort of unwelcome invisibility" (2009, 18). In our programs, "nothing to say" includes not having popular possessions like toys, books, or light-up shoes; insufficient knowledge of significant scripts from movies or books; lacking the ability to navigate the monkey bars or run fast; and not sharing experiences such as vacations and trips to amusement parks. Children arrive in our early care spaces with vast differences in these elements, and those differences can be a source of distance between children.

Pugh coined the phrase "economy of dignity" to describe this concept of securing belonging in the community. "Children collect or confer dignity among themselves, according to their (shifting) consensus about what sort of objects or experiences are supposed to count for it" (7). For children, she argues, the most basic desire is to be "worthy of belonging." Children who have dignity are granted "the very right to speak in their own community's conversation" (7). It is important to note that dignity carries the idea of esteem rather than envy. Through the material things of childhood, children are trying to sit in their circle of peers, not trying to prove themselves better than their peers. Counter to the culture of adulthood, there is no need to compete, only a need to belong.

The Power of Material Things

Very often, when children bring toys from home into the child care space, those toys can be a problem. Looking through the lens of belonging, it's clear that part of the reason these toys are such a challenge is that they represent a threat to belonging. The issue of material possessions is a difficult one in early childhood spaces. Should providers prohibit children from bringing toys from home? Possibly. I know I worried about what might happen if children brought their own toys from home—the inequality that might surface, the possibility that I might find those toys problematic, as well as the danger that those things might get lost or damaged. In reality, though, banning toys from home doesn't really solve the problems children face with belonging, because those problems might stem from anything the child brings, like a pair of light-up shoes.

One May, Cassy arrived wearing new light-up tennis shoes that she promptly promenaded with a speedy sprint around the room. As she bolted from one wall to the other and back again, she decreed her title as the fastest in the room, a title held exclusively by wearers of light-up shoes. This posed a problem for her best friend, Isobel, who watched mystified as her other half ran in circles around her. With the declaration that superlative speed was tied to a multicolored flashing LED light, Isobel would never be the fastest; her shoes were ordinary brown leather with Velcro straps and a pattern of flowers stitched into the side. Isobel felt a threat to her sense of belonging.

When the whole group gathered for breakfast, I noticed a familiar flash of anger in Isobel's eyes. She was emotionally turbulent. With thunderous emotional clouds on the horizon, we began a group discussion of feelings as I attempted to stave off the F5 hurricane that would surely follow if Isobel were left alone in her place of sadness. The two four-year-olds verbalized their version of the morning's athletic display, some tears were shed, and I sensed the clouds dissipating. Several minutes later, after the conversation had wound its way around all manner of other important topics—daily plans, ideas about frogs, and a rousing round of "The Wheels on the Bus"—Isobel spontaneously reached across the table, grabbed Cassy's bowl of cereal, and dumped the whole thing out.

Apparently, resolution was incomplete.

Soggy flakes scattered like islands amidst the pooling milk, which ran between the crack in the leaf of the table and onto Cassy's skirt. She exploded. Meanwhile, the nine-month-old at the table was absolutely overcome by the circus of fitful screaming and people rushing to contain the milk river. Pleased with the chaos, he joined the party by emptying the contents of my cereal bowl (serendipitously left within arm's reach) and began to splash with glee. Following some quick paper towel work, the whole mess was cleaned up in a relative flash. But the fire of Isobel's great anger had not yet flared into its final display. Slightly less than three minutes later, she grabbed another child's milk cup and dumped it out, eyes locked on mine as the last drops dripped from the cup onto the newly dried table.

The culture of adulthood sees behaviors like young Isobel's as defiance, her actions a thrown gauntlet awaiting my swift and strong reply. In this respect, I appreciate the wisdom of Margie Carter, who writes in an article about toddler behavior that approaching young ones with "a mindset of curiosity rather than compliance can begin to transform our responses" (2008, 39). This ability to be curious stands in defiant opposition to the demands of a behaviorist's "you get what you pay for" approach. As educators, we are encouraged to look at Isobel in the context of her whole experience, recognizing her milk dumping as evidence of a significant wound. Her best friend resided in a camp of "fast runners," and she was not invited. Scarcity defined her place as an outsider at the breakfast table, and she desperately sought a way back, screaming for attention so she would know that she belonged.

The solution to the problem of Isobel and Cassy is not prohibiting the light-up tennis shoes, though that might appear to solve the problem in the short run. The solution is not in distancing Isobel further through punishments for her milk-dumping displays, even though they seem—in our tit-for-tat economic understanding of life—to be solidly warranted. After all, milk is expensive! She wasted something of value, and in the economics of adulthood, I deserve something of value (her time, her apologies) in return. But the culture of childhood is different. The challenge is to speak within her cultural framework to help Isobel regain a sense of belonging in her community despite different shoes.

On the day of the great breakfast milk river, we started by verbalizing the possibility of wearing different shoes and remaining friends, voicing feelings of hurt and disappointment, and truly helping Isobel and Cassy reconnect through time and play. Isobel's wound was so great that she needed help to find connection with Cassy once again. I set out some playdough—Isobel's preferred sensory activity—and began to play. Soon she joined in, and Cassy, lured equally by the strong pull of the soft dough, followed shortly after. I stayed at the table long enough to establish a loose play structure, but before long both girls were pulled into a play rhythm of their own design. They belonged at that table together.

Ultimately, I don't think there is one prescriptive rule that works for all spaces regarding material things. Some programs allow children to bring things from home while others do not. Some even find a midway point where children can bring possessions but must leave them in their cubbies during the day, possibly bringing them out at naptime. Often, the particular needs of the children involved come into play when deciding on these policies. A child who is having a difficult time separating might find some comfort from bringing an object to day care every day. Regardless of the particular stance educators take regarding children's personal material possessions, we must be aware of the role those items play from within the economic system of the culture of childhood.

The Power of Knowledge and Experience

Once the children in my family child care program were pretending to be characters from a cartoon. Among the playing cohort, only one of the girls had actually seen the cartoon, so getting the play started was incredibly difficult. Her ideas were in constant conflict with those of her peers, because she had a road map none of her friends could see. She immediately claimed the role of the platypus.

"I want to be a platypus, too!" said her friend.

"You can't. There's only one platypus."

My attempts to support the script by adding another platypus or additional characters were tossed aside. I didn't have the currency to purchase a place in the script. The following scenarios show similar economic breakdowns:

- After a week camping with family in Colorado, two-year-old Ruby plays camping. Her friend Luke has never been camping, so he keeps messing up the order of setting up the tent. Ruby gets frustrated and abandons the play.

- At the art table, four five-year-old boys are working hard to draw a robot from a popular children's show. One boy, who does not watch the show, colors the shirt green instead of red, like the one in the show. The others notice, saying, "Robots can't have a green shirt!"

- Mina starts her first day at a new child care program. When she arrives, she is greeted by three other girls who ask, "Who is your favorite princess?" Mina doesn't have a favorite princess, to which the other girls simply say, "Oh," and they go on playing without her.

Knowledge of relevant scripts can be a way for children to find belonging with one another, but such scripts can also cause problems for children who don't share the same knowledge. As early childhood educators, we can help children find places of belonging. Since all children arrive with different possessions, experiences, and knowledge, our programs need to be rich in opportunities for children to create new experiences of commonality:

- Open-ended, noncommercial materials invite children of all knowledge bases to create.

- Ample blocks of time give children opportunities to accommodate each other in novel scripts.

- Talking with children directly about what it feels like to belong and to be left out helps provide children with language to use to share relevant experiences.

Finding Belonging

As they get older, children develop a strong sense of the way to secure belonging. Like young Bryan, slowing his speed so that Esther could play, children find creative ways to use things, experiences, abilities, and knowledge in order to "purchase" belonging. My three children play remarkably well together. They find synchronicity more often than not, and develop complicated story lines that carry from day to day. The year my oldest daughter entered first grade created a challenging dynamic. Homework. Each night, she would come home with a few minutes of schoolwork, and during this time, the other two children often settled into a play rhythm. When the oldest would try and insert herself into the game that was already under way, she often found that her brother and sister were less inclined to include her.

One day, after her homework was finished, she said to me, "Isn't it time for a snack?"

"Oh yes. I forgot," I replied. "I'll get it ready right now."

"No, I'll do it, Mom." I was surprised by her initiative. She set the table with plates, fruit, and cheese and asked for something sweet. I consented. Then she went to her brother and sister, who were well involved in play. She listened at the door of their bedroom for a moment and overheard a script involving horses. She opened the door and assumed a character. "Hi, horses. I have a horse snack ready for you at the stable. It is strawberries, cheese, and a cookie."

I smiled. She had purchased a spot in the game.

This act was not manipulative. She was using sophisticated skills of empathy to consider what her brother and sister would want, as well as attending to the content of the script before looking for a point of entry in order to make an attempt at belonging. She knew with each added element—a snack *plus* something sweet—she had a better chance of being included.

Toddler culture is a fabulous example of this kind of economic transaction. In chapter 2, I gave an example of repetitive toddler play, and I'd like to return to that example for a moment. Recall the story of the three young toddlers who were sitting together at a dining room table banging plates as a game. In this game, each child was allowed to participate because each child had the materials (a plastic plate) and the means (the capacity to bang the plate on the table). If children had an adult concept of material objects, fueled by competition, the experience might look different. Someone would add a sophisticated pounding pattern. Someone else might add a clapping routine. Another person might begin to sing a song. Over time, the experience would morph into something that was restricted to only the most talented and capable percussionists. By contrast, the toddlers banged their plates until someone else shifted the routine, but the shift was subtle, and it was one that could accommodate the skill level of all the children involved.

The same kinds of interactions happen among children of slightly different skill levels. In multiage settings, one of the great joys is to watch the interactions between age-groups. The older children cherish a chance to teach the younger children new skills. One afternoon, Lacy (seventeen months) was trying to fit a series of blocks into a shape sorter. Gabriela (two and a half years) was watching Lacy struggle to push a triangle into the square hole. She walked over to Lacy and pointed to the triangle hole. "Lacy. Here. Here." Lacy reoriented the focus of her attention toward getting the triangle into the triangle hole. Both girls worked together to get all the shapes in their proper place. Older children are very eager to share their skills with younger children. In part, this is because in giving information to their peers, the children get to share experiences together. What a powerful image! I think about how this kind of narrative would transform the kinds of interactions that are so typical in competitive fields. In graduate school, colleagues would be sharing articles with one another with a note: "Thought you might find this research helpful!"

Scarcity in the Culture of Childhood: Separating from Loved Ones

Children have a different experience with scarcity. For adults, scarcity typically refers to resources and time, but for children, the scarcity they experience relates to their sense of belonging to their community. One way this awareness of scarcity manifests itself in child care settings is during times of separation. Consider Daniel. He does not want to spend the day at child care. For the entire twenty-minute walk from his house to his school, he pleads with his father: "Why do I have to go to school? I don't want to go to school. I don't like school. The slide is too short. I don't get to paint." He rattles off objection after objection while his father listens attentively.

When they arrive, Daniel is reticent. He grabs tightly to his father's leg as he helps Daniel change his shoes for indoor play. He begins to cry. "I don't want to go to school. I don't want you to leave me! Stay with me!"

His father's heart breaks. He knows that Daniel enjoys school, and is often reluctant to leave at the end of the day. The process of leaving is painful for everyone involved. His father puts his arms around Daniel for one final squeeze, and hands him off to his teacher, who comes lovingly alongside the sad separation and holds him in her arms. Daniel wrestles to get free, but she calmly and gently assures him: "Daddy will come back. Good-bye, Daddy. We'll see you later."

Daniel is lucky to have a teacher who knows how to speak his language. She tells him with calm, reassuring words, "Daddy will come back. You will play today at school, eat lunch, have a rest time, and then Daddy will come back."

Other children have gathered because of Daniel's heavy sobs. His teacher narrates for the onlookers. "Daniel is sad because his daddy left. I'm sad, too, when people that I love have to leave." Several children nod in agreement, the raised eyebrows of concern showing a deep and empathic connection to his emotions. "Sometimes, it helps me to have a picture of the people that I love. I wonder if Daniel would like to have his family picture?" Without waiting for Daniel to respond, one of the children in the ring breaks away quickly to retrieve the basket of family pictures. He finds the one of Daniel with his father and pet dog.

"I wonder what else might be comforting to Daniel. I know when I am sad, sometimes it helps to sit with people who love me and read a book," offers his teacher.

"I like my blanket," replies one child.

"I like my bear," says another.

The children disperse, gathering special items from around the room: a stuffed animal from the soft corner and a blanket from the dress-up area. Tomás even brings his own comfort blanket from his cubbie to offer Daniel. The children crouch close to Daniel; he has stopped crying but is still deeply sad. They begin to talk sweetly to him, asking what would be helpful, and inviting him to be close to them while he's sad.

Daniel gathers his peers' offerings with tender gratitude and climbs into his teacher's lap. After a few minutes together, the teacher suggests another strategy for soothing the pain of separation: "Another thing that helps me sometimes is to write a note to the people that I miss." The children think this is a fantastic idea, and everyone, with pictures of their loved ones in tow, huddles around the table to dictate letters. Daniel's reads: "Dear Daddy, I miss you. I'm sad. I am crying lots of tears. Raphael has a truck shirt. I love you. Love, Daniel."

Times of separation are challenging for young children, because the parting signals a threat to their sense of belonging. Can they belong to two communities simultaneously? This sense of scarcity flows through their bodies like the blood in their veins, occupying their subconscious and preventing them from truly relaxing into the moment. For children, belonging is expressed through presence, and they lack the life experience to know how each separation will resolve. In addition, the child's perception of time makes each moment feel excruciatingly *present*; the fact that Mommy or Daddy will return means nothing because they are gone *now*.

Early childhood educators can help children with painful moments of scarcity related to separation by reevaluating two particularly unhelpful practices associated with pickup and drop-off times. The first is the practice of sneaking away from children. Families find separations as painful as their children. They don't like to see their children cry, and they worry that they are doing something wrong when their children are so upset. To protect their children, adults often sneak away. They make sure their children are deeply engaged in an activity, and then they make a break for the door before their children notice anything is different. These well-intentioned adults are misguided. Sneaking away leaves children feeling afraid and worried that their loved ones can't be trusted. Over time, children can develop a suspicious disposition. They will resist leaving their parents to get involved in anything for fear that their parents will go away when they aren't looking.

A second practice that we must reconsider is distracting children when they are upset about a separation. Adults—parents and caregivers alike—often operate with the flawed belief that in distracting children from the sadness, we are helping them settle in to play. When families leave their children in our care, practitioners often feel the need to stop the children from crying as quickly as possible. We grow more animated, we reach for sparkly and compelling toys, we rock young babies on our laps with a fantastic fervor, and we ply older children with the promise of snacktime. "Don't worry. Mommy will be back soon. *Ooooooohhh! Did* you *see* this *monkey?* Where is the monkey? *Here it is!* Peek-a-boo! Look over here! See? Oh, don't cry. Look! Find the monkey!"

We mean well, but our attempts to quiet children who are upset sometimes stem from our own discomfort with strong feelings. Often, adults feel very uncomfortable in the presence of a child's strong feelings, and a child care provider with a whole group of small children to care for can easily feel overwhelmed by the long-lasting cries of a child who feels the pain of separation. Child care providers often worry about what others might think if they see a child crying. Will other families or colleagues think I'm not doing a good job if I can't get the children to stop crying?

A child who is distracted will likely quiet down, and possibly more quickly than a child who is not distracted and enticed to leave her lookout point by the window. We fall into a trap of using crying as a gauge. If a child is crying, there's something wrong I need to fix. When the crying is done, the problem is solved. But crying is a poor gauge of resolution. Even though the absence might be less potent to the outside world, children's minds remain occupied with that sense of loss, preventing them from fully engaging with peers.

Distracting children with toys teaches them to disconnect and distract from their strong feelings, communicating to children that their pain and sorrow is less important than their happy engagement with the world around them. Educator Kelly Matthews says, "Toys serve as emotional distractions, and if children don't learn to manage strong emotional feelings when they are young in healthy ways, what things will substitute for toys as children grow up?" (Matthews 2015). Children have a right to be upset when their loved ones leave, and when we resist the urge to pacify their crying with cheap substitutes for human connection, we communicate that their sense of connection to their community is important.

Helping Children Separate from Loved Ones

When it comes to children and the pain of separating, we need to reconnect with the sense of loss that children experience. We know that the end of the day will come, and that parents will return, but we rush too quickly to that happy reunion instead of attending to the moment with children who are sad. As we feel an increased sense of empathy for the children in our care who are sad, we can more effectively help them navigate their strong emotions:

> **Anticipate challenging days and challenging times of day.**
> The first days back after a holiday, the days after a new child begins care, and morning drop-off time are predictably challenging for young ones. Make breakfast in advance and have it ready to serve. Create a warm and peaceful environment to greet children. Prepare the play area so that children who feel comfortable can begin playing independently so you have time to tend to specific children.

> **Acknowledge their feelings.** Move close to children who are sad and use phrases that reveal your understanding. "You are sad. You wish Mommy didn't have to leave."

> **Connect.** Children need to know that they aren't alone. "When I leave the people I love, it makes me sad, too." Other children may gather to share their own expressions of empathy, through their facial expressions, their body language, and their gifts.

Extend an offer to help. "When I leave the ones I love, it helps sometimes if I have a hug. Would you like a hug? Would you like to sit with me? Would you like a cool washcloth for your face?" Our offers can be creative.

If you must transition to other activities (breakfast, for example) be clear with the child. "It's time for me to get breakfast out at the table. Would you like to sit next to me? Would you like to sit facing the door? Would you like to bring a picture of your mommy with you to the table?"

Helping Families Separate from their Children

Early child care educators must find ways to reassure families about the process of separating. Children will commonly experience phases of heightened separation anxiety that peak at predictable times in their development. Even if families have maintained a strong connection with a single early care provider, and even if young children have had no prior issues with separation, many will enter a period of reluctance to leave their parents between nine months and eighteen months, and again between ages two and three. These periods coincide with the development of specific cognitive leaps and are challenging to manage.

Early childhood educators should anticipate this time and reassure families that it is normal. Often, families become worried if their children start crying all of a sudden. They wonder if something has changed in the program, and they worry that their children aren't happy. Make a phone call in the evening, or protect time at the end of the day to talk with families about this phase of development. Sending short text messages or photos of their child having fun during the day can also be reassuring for families.

Communicate expectations about a drop-off routine. Children find predictability reassuring, so develop and communicate a policy about how families can help with the transitions to and from care. Preparing a letter to communicate your philosophy is helpful. Families need to know that by sticking with the same routine every day and by following through with what they say they are going to do, they help their children develop trust in the process of saying good-bye.

Keeping Children Connected

Beyond soothing children and educating families, early childhood professionals can maximize the opportunities for young children to stay connected to their home communities during a day of child care, affirming to children that they belong to several communities at once:

- As part of the enrollment packet, ask families to provide pictures of loved ones (parents, siblings, relatives, neighbors, babysitters, pets, significant places from home). Laminate these pictures and place them in a basket, or make them into a small flip book for the child to carry around. Children in my program would often bring their family pictures to mealtimes so they could eat with their loved ones, and sleep with their family pictures at naptime.

- Letter writing is a powerful tool to help children stay connected. Keep paper, pens or pencils, and envelopes available at all times and offer to transcribe a dictated letter for a sad child.

- Model the process for children. Keep pictures of your own loved ones close at hand. When you are having a difficult day, reach for your pictures to model the process for children.

The Currency of Childhood: Attention

When we think about children and attention, our thoughts often revolve around a child having a tantrum on the floor, and an adult calmly observing, "Oh, she's just trying to get attention." American society believes that children are manipulative, doing what they can to swindle our undeserved attention like a con artist luring an unsuspecting victim. When we adults "cave" to the children's poor behavior by attending to the children, we are pawns in their game. This is wrong. We misunderstand childhood behavior because of our cultural "get what you deserve" bias. Society believes that because a child's negative behaviors are attention seeking, the best response and the simplest way to "train" a child to behave properly is to ignore those behaviors. This is a colossal misunderstanding of childhood culture.

Attention is a difficult hurdle for adults. We are so deeply enmeshed in the narrative that "you get what you pay for" that extending attention to a child as a fundamental right of her humanity, despite her behavior, seems impossible. The call to recognize the culture of childhood is an echoing cry for a change in this paradigm. Attention is not a tool of manipulation. Attention is a piece of the equation whereby children know they belong to the community around them.

Pretend to be a child. You are three feet tall, and when your mother comes to pick you up from your day at school, she greets you and then turns her attention to your teacher. While they stand and talk, you don't even know if they see you because you stand far below their eye level. They don't make eye contact with you, they don't talk to you (though they sometimes talk about you), and they don't play with you. These are two of the most important people in your world, and you don't even know if they are aware of you. How do you know you still have a place in the community? What clues exist that tell you that you matter? If one of the foundational markers of your sense of belonging is attention, and your sense of belonging is critical to your understanding of value, then how do you know you haven't become invisible to the people you love? You might try to confirm that you still matter by trying to get their attention. You say your mother's name over and over, you tap her on the legs, you run into her with all your weight, and you grab her hands and pull them while you run around her body in circles. She ignores you; acts like you aren't even there. Finally, when she does respond, she's not happy but irritated, snapping something about not interrupting and "waiting just a few minutes."

As adults, our gentlest responses to a child's calls for attention are loving reminders, such as, "I'll be there in just a minute." For children, the present is so critically important. The future is not something they have much experience with, so this act of waiting is a hard task for very little ones. Their calls for attention might escalate; their behaviors might grow grander and louder. What we must understand is that this is because their sense of urgency is increasing as they wait. Just recently, my son was crying about a sore in his mouth where he had bitten his cheek. He was crying about how it really hurt, and I offered to look into his mouth with a flashlight. "Oh, it's just a sore. It will heal soon," I told him. His response reminded me that "soon" is a tough qualifier for a three-year-old to grasp, and "just a sore" belittles the significance of his experience: "But Mom! It maybe will hurt for my *whole life*!" He doesn't conceive of injuries in terms of degree, only in terms of presence. He might solicit the same level of attention for a cut on the knee or a broken limb because in that moment, that particular injury is as real as any other, past or future, and he lacks confidence that it will heal. When a child is unsure of her sense of belonging, when she perceives that attention is scarce, she will do whatever she can to reestablish attention as quickly as possible. The scarcity she feels is the same scarcity I feel when I lose my money. It overwhelms me and consumes my mental energy until I find it again.

When we realize these calls for what they are—reminders to the child that he matters, that he is valuable, that he has a meaningful place in the community—it can shape our responses. Children who are asking for attention, regardless of the manner in which they are asking, need attention. Giving a child attention, even when he doesn't "deserve" it, is one of the most countercultural acts early childhood educators can do. Let me give you an example of what this looks like in practice.

My four-year-old daughter was one of the children in my in-home program when two-year-old Hallie joined our group. At the end of each day, Hallie's four-year-old brother, Marcus, came along with his mother at pickup time. Hallie's mom and I enjoyed a slow end-of-the-day routine with ten to fifteen minutes of visiting time while our children played together. Marcus became one of the group. He loved the new environment and materials and was eager to engage with a new set of peers, but my daughter wasn't so thrilled. Her difficult behaviors started off mildly—games of tag, orchestrated so that Marcus was always "it," or play scripts with no room left for him to join. Over time, the behaviors escalated to small kicks, hair pulling, pushing, and teasing. With every incident, I felt embarrassed; this was *my* program and *my* daughter was overwhelmingly unwelcoming and unkind. Fortunately, Hallie's mom was also an early childhood educator, and she and I worked together to problem solve the situation.

Times of transition can be very destabilizing for young children, and for my daughter, it was no different. I suspected that her behavior during the daily pickup resulted from a threat to her sense of belonging: she felt insecure because my attention was divided. She was asking me, through her loud and unkind behavior, if she still mattered. Everything in my body wanted to distance myself (and the rest of the children) from her in those inappropriate moments to teach her that that was not how you got attention, but entering her cultural understanding gave me new eyes to see the dilemma she faced. I still protected the emotional and physical safety all of the children involved, but I did it in a way that preserved my daughter's sense of value and belonging with myself and her peers.

Outside of the moment, my daughter and I talked about the transition at the end of the day and how I noticed that she had a hard time when Marcus arrived. I wondered aloud about tools that might help her through those moments. We talked about how everyone had a right to feel welcome and safe in our space, and about how we all had to work together to make sure that happened. Together, we devised a plan for pickup time, one that included empowering her to be friendly as well as alerting her to the upcoming transition. Hallie's mom arrived at a predictable time every day, so I was able to give my daughter some advance notice about Marcus's arrival. We talked at length about the power present in relationships, and I drew her attention to the fact that she held the power to make Marcus feel welcome and included. I also verbalized for her the reality of my divided attention during those moments.

I gave her tools to "hold on" to me during those moments of perceived distance—she could come stand close and hold my hand, she could wear one of my bracelets, she could place a picture of me in the play space where it would be close as she was playing, and most of all, if she needed my attention, she could ask for it in ways that kept her peers safe. We devised a signal, something she could use if she was desperate. She could come and grab my pinky. When I felt her grab my pinky, I would pause my conversation and give her my attention. I explained that I could not respond to this signal often, that I needed to give attention to the adults who were coming to pick up their children. We agreed that the signal must be reserved for injuries or similar problems that absolutely could not wait. With the safety of a lifeline to me, she felt powerful again, and she used that power as a force for kindness when Marcus arrived. And, as the days went on, she never used the pinky lifeline.

The kind of attention children need is very specific. There is unhelpful attention that comes along with the pressure to perform, like when children are put on the spot to show off a new skill ("Show Emily how you can count to ten!"), or when children engage in competitive performance activities. These experiences can put pressure on kids to behave in certain ways, and that pressure can actually perpetuate a sense of disconnection. Some children enjoy these kinds of experiences, but they are not, in this sense, attention-renewing experiences. Another unhelpful attention is a persistent and watchful attention. When children are watched at every moment, they grow dependent on our approval and permission for everything they do. This type of attention communicates a lack of trust or confidence in children's ability to do things on their own.

Another problem with attention is that sometimes we think we are giving attention when we aren't. Children live with the reality that their parents and other significant adults are perpetually distracted. Cell phones chime when new e-mails or text messages arrive, and wireless Internet allows us to remain connected to work and other obligations perpetually. Children are in regular competition for attention, not only with peers, but now also with technology. The kind of attention children crave is an undivided, single-focused attention.

Finally, learning to wait—even though it is excruciatingly difficult—is a critical task for young children. It's helpful to remember that children who are showing a need for attention will not—in those moments of attention-seeking behavior—be ready to learn the skill of waiting. Teaching children to wait is important, but human beings can't learn if their sense of value is threatened. After children feel connected, we can help give them tools to learn to wait.

Here are some examples for managing attention-seeking behaviors:

Pickup time. Joseph's mother comes to pick him up from school. His mother and I review the day while Joseph bounces nearby. He begins to yell, "Emily! Emily! Emily!" I pause my story with his mother, bend down so Joseph and I are looking into each other's eyes, and tell him, "I want to hear what you need to say. I am talking to your mom, so I can't give you my attention now. Hold my hand so you don't forget that you have something to say, and as soon as I'm done, you can tell me." I then resume talking to his mom while he holds on to my hand.

Staying still. One of the best things we can do to help children feel secure and develop a sense of belonging is to stay in one place. Literally. At the park, find a bench to sit on and tell all of the children, "If you need me, I will be right here." While the children are playing in the morning, dedicate twenty minutes to sitting in proximity to the children and working on a project of your own (such as reading a book). Spend some time playing with the children, but be sure to protect time during the day for the children to play with each other without your constant hovering. Allow for spaces that are semi private where you are still able to supervise, but children have a sense of aloneness. Think about spots behind furniture or under a staircase that are otherwise unused and decorate these small nooks and crannies for children to use.

Unplug. Keeping a cell phone close is helpful for important parent communication and in the event of an emergency. Plus, I like having a camera always available! But remember to silence your cell phone and turn notifications off so the beeping and notifications won't take you out of the moment.

Be specific. Tell children exactly what they can do to get your attention, and exactly how attention works. "I need to finish listening to Ella before I can listen fully to you." "When you have something to tell me, but I'm talking to someone else, you have to wait until I'm done to start talking. Come and touch my hand so I know you have something to say."

Wrapping It Up

Understanding the motivations behind our behaviors is powerful. Knowing that children try to get attention because they sense a threat to their sense of belonging might change the way we choose to respond. Seeing how distracting a child from the pain of separating might threaten her sense of security in the child care community might challenge us to rethink our typical responses. Watching for the ways in which children modulate their ability to foster belonging, or noticing the hurt that children feel when they don't have the same toys as their peers shifts our responses. In this chapter, as in all the others, the goal is that our attitudes and behavior toward children change, that we build in an awareness of the significance of the work that children are doing.

Stories from the Field

TEATIME

by Marc Battle

It was in a child care, many years ago, that I learned a valuable lesson about belonging. I was working on the island of Haida Gwaii, an archipelago on the North Coast of British Columbia, in a classroom with children who ranged in age from three to five.

I began to notice a pattern in the accident reports: most of the injuries that occurred during a day happened during the last hour of care. I began to wonder why, and thought about what a child might experience during that hour of care. From the child's perspective, that last hour can feel like forever; like they are never going to be picked up. They see their peers going home and still no one has come for them. The younger ones, lacking experience with the routine of daily pickup time, are not even 100 percent sure that they are even being picked up at all.

I knew that if I wanted to ease whatever was going on during this time I would have to come up with something that tied us together, marking our time together as something special, and creating a community of belonging. Then it hit me. Teatime.

When I was young, I use to go to my grandmother's apartment after school with my younger brother, and we would sit together and have tea and talk. Sometimes the neighbors would join us and we would hear all of the gossip and goings-on that were happening in the apartment block. It was a special time for me. I felt like I was reuniting with my community and that I belonged in that place.

These children, at the end of their day, needed the same thing. With petty cash in hand I headed to the grocery store to buy organic, noncaffeinated, herbal peppermint tea and eight unbreakable teacups. When the last hour arrived I announced, "Hey, everybody. Let's clean up and have some tea in real tea cups." "Real tea?" a child asked. "Real herbal tea," I replied. They busily cleaned up and set the cups on the table while I brewed the tea. After adding some cold water to cool it down, we all sat together and I poured the peppermint tea.

I thought I would use this moment to read a book, but a child stopped me and asked, "Could we just talk instead?" He was right and we talked. We spent every last hour during my time with them drinking tea and talking about all of the goings-on in the preschool room.

No more accidents, just a special time together.

Marc Battle is an ECE instructor at Red River College in Winnipeg, Manitoba. He is also a noted children's musician and adventure playground developer.

"No One Remains Unchanged"
Transformation

"Bridging differences is ultimately a transformational process. When we first recognize and acknowledge our interdependence, we experience a shift in our view of our relationships from 'us-them' to 'we.'"

—Nike Carstarphen

WITHOUT A CULTURE OF CHILDHOOD, children will always be simply *un*-adults: unable to navigate social interactions without oversight, lacking linguistic fluency, relying on worlds of fantasy instead of existing in reality, inefficient in production, and unaware of a concept of worth or value. Adults are trained to think in terms of forming the unformed child, to socializing the savage toddler, and forcing compliance in the obstinate young child. Every interaction, from the activities we offer to the ways in which we speak to children, is assessed by its value on the child as a future adult. Sociologist David Goode offers this scathing indictment of a society that fails to recognize the validity of a childhood culture: "In a sense . . . most of our knowledge about children is missionary-like, largely because adults are culturally in the position of domination and conversion. And like missionaries, we have legitimacy up front on our side, and we do not have to acknowledge or concern ourselves with the natives' beliefs in order to get the job of conversion (that is, socialization) done" (1994, 168). How true! In the current adult culture, children are always valuable and supported to the extent that they are becoming adults.

Some will argue that children—who one day will be adults—must have the skills to enter adulthood, and therefore, as early childhood educators, we have a responsibility to teach children acceptable ways of being adults. Hitting to get a toy from a peer, for example, is not a suitable way to be an adult, and adults have a responsibility to conform a child's behavior to acceptable adult norms. It's important to state that the culture of childhood does not stand in opposition to the process of growing up. As children age and interact with their peer cohort and the adults around them, they will develop the socially appropriate tools of their same-aged peers, but foundational to the child's ability to grow into a successful adult is the use of culturally relevant tools and structures to make sense of the world through their unique perspectives. In the same way that I wouldn't purchase clothes three sizes too big in anticipation of a day when I might need larger clothing, or I wouldn't start walking with crutches in case I break my leg, I don't teach children to sit because they will one day be in kindergarten, or demand that they "use their words" when communicating through play is their natural means of communicating. Embracing childhood as its own unique culture forces us to step into the lives of children for the human beings they are in the *present*, trusting that they will grow into the adults they are in the process of becoming.

This book has offered a bold understanding and defense of childhood. Instead of seeing children as the passive beings that adults are responsible for shaping, children are active members of their own vibrant culture. They possess their own unique ways of interacting with and making sense of the world. Early childhood educators have an important duty to understand the functions of childhood pursuits. We recognize the means by which young children form friendships. We know that children communicate and make meaning in the world through play, both tame and wild. We understand the deep significance of embracing a process-oriented approach, and we understand how children conceive of value in terms of love and belonging.

The meeting of two cultures is known as the process of acculturation. When I moved to Switzerland, I was faced with a culture that looked different from my home culture of the United States. On the surface, I was faced with the most obvious difference—language. Underneath the language were many other differences—expectations about dress, consumption, politeness, and appropriate topics of conversation, to name just a few. I was faced with a dilemma of how to interact within a new culture.

In cultural studies literature, individuals respond in several ways to the collision between their native culture and one that is foreign. I could *assimilate*, meaning I could shed my American identity, speak French exclusively at home and in public, and adopt as many of the cultural norms of my new Swiss community as possible. Over time, my connection to the United States would diminish, and my future family tree would be more Swiss than American. A second strategy I could use would be to *separate*. In separating, I would stay in my apartment in Switzerland, make friends with other English-speaking immigrants, and remain on my little American island in this new country of residence. I would still have cordial, polite contact with the Swiss, but those points of contact would be distant, and I would still value my cultural norms above those of my host culture. A third choice for me would be to *integrate*: I could cultivate having a foot in both worlds, maintaining my own English and the English language of my children while gaining fluency in French. I would value my traditions while learning about the traditions of Switzerland.

The process of acculturation affects many different interactions. At the bus stop near my house in Switzerland last spring, I had a chance encounter with a neighbor. The weather was warming up, though it was chilly and summer was still far away. Regardless, my feet had been subjected to socks and shoes for far too many months, and I was wearing sandals. I was a little cold, but so grateful for my toes to be free. My neighbor smiled and pointed to my feet. "You're not worried you're going to get sick?" I wasn't. In fact, wearing sandals in chilly weather never put me at risk of getting sick when I was living in the United States, because the link between sockless toes and illness was not part of my cultural upbringing.

A few days later, I was presented with the same opportunity. It was a sunny day, warm enough (in my mind) for sandals, but not warm enough by Swiss standards. The process of acculturation influences many life decisions: I could wear closed-toed shoes as a symbol of my assimilation; I could wear sandals as a symbol of my separation, judging the Swiss belief about illness and cold feet as a position of inferiority; or I could wear my sandals as a practice of integration, carrying my American culture while remaining sensitive and respectful to the Swiss point of view. In time, my neighbor would be faced with the same decisions. She could see my American sandal-wearing self as an invitation to try something culturally foreign. At the very least, she would be challenged to rethink her perspective on sandals in springtime, if for no other reason than to remember her cultural commitments.

David Sam and John Berry, professors of psychology at universities in Norway and Canada, respectively, wrote an article describing the process of acculturation. "No cultural group," they assert, "remains unchanged following culture contact; acculturation is a two-way interaction" (2010, 473). Our job as early childhood educators is to see our work with young children as an experience of acculturation, of sorts. Children change as a result of their interaction with the culture of adulthood, but adults also change as they encounter the culture of childhood. Many of the problems we experience are the result of our having chosen the path of assimilation rather than integration. We have cut ties with our former childhood selves, and we no longer have the capacity to play, to engage in make-believe, to separate our worth from a product, or to find value in belonging. We no longer have the tools of our former childhood selves, so we are inefficient when it comes to nurturing the children in our care. We have an opportunity to choose the path of integration, benefiting not only children but adults as well. Adults who retain some of the cultural tools of childhood have deep capacities for creativity, flexible thinking, and defining their lives by the quality of relationships. In choosing integration, we welcome the process of transformation that happens when we encounter the culture of childhood.

Inviting Transformation

At the start of this book, I offered an invitation to hold on to the *surprise* that comes when we move from being "tourists" to become "culturally aware outsiders." And now, I invite you to experience the transformation that takes place when we step into that role.

Viewing childhood as a culture gives children the right to claim childhood as their identity, to build a society with the foundational belief that childhood is not a state of *incompleteness* nor a state of *almost*. The human beings who form the culture of childhood are competent and complex, deserving of a community that will celebrate their culture and encourage them to live whole and full lives. As early childhood educators, we have the ability to transform social thinking about young children, and it all begins with understanding childhood as a distinct culture. As we adopt practices of care that are culturally sensitive, we become unique allies for young children. Children need adults who will look at behaviors as evidence of a need, adults who will suspend judgment and adopt a posture of surprise and curiosity about those needs, and adults who will advocate for the rights of children to experience life as children rather than as deficient adults.

We have an invitation to enter our own transformation; no one remains unchanged. Our children are not mini-adults, neither are they stationed at a precivilized point on the continuum of human development. They inhabit a distinct worldview and mind-set. When we honor this mind-set in the same manner that we would honor the mind-set of someone from a different culture, we enter into a dialogue with children that is supremely respectful and integrated, and we teach them to do the same with other people. Through this process, we too are changed.

Group Discussion Guide

THANK YOU FOR READING *Discovering the Culture of Childhood*. I prepared this discussion guide to help enrich your reading experience. I designed it specifically for use in small reading groups, as I think the best way to process some of the information in this book is with a reading partner. That said, individuals reading alone can certainly use the guide. If you are interested, I invite you to consider starting a reading group. If you need help connecting with other interested readers in your area, I have a page called "Start a Reading Group" on my website that gives you ideas regarding how to get one started. If you have a reading group and you would like to invite me to join one of your meetings via video conference, I would be happy to do that! Visit my website, emilyplank.com, for more information.

These questions were written primarily with practitioners in mind. Therefore, some questions assume readers are actively working with children in the field of early childhood education. I understand that some of you may be students, parents, administrators, support professionals, policy makers, and others. If you find a question that doesn't seem applicable to you, I invite you to use your imagination to consider a situation in which the question might apply. Maybe you are raising your own children, or you have experience as a nanny, or you used to work in a child care program, or you can imagine what it might be like to be part of such a program.

Good luck, and happy discussing!

Introduction. "Becoming Outsiders": An Invitation

1. Have you had an experience when you thought of yourself as an outsider? What memories stand out?

2. Our use of adult language to describe the behaviors of young children influences clothing manufacturers. I have seen T-shirts and onesies for babies and toddlers with messages that carry double meanings—one applicable to the culture of childhood and one imported from the culture of adulthood. (A baby onesie with the phrase "I drink until I pass out" alongside an image of a bottle, for example.) Have you seen such clothing? Describe the messages you saw.

Chapter 1. "It's a Good Thing You're Fat!": Why Culture Matters

1. Take a moment to reflect on your own cultural identity. Some elements you might consider include your age, place of residence, place of birth, ability level, family structure, gender, sexual orientation, socioeconomic status, and occupation. Some of these elements will be defining aspects of your identity while others will not.

2. What types of behaviors would be in your *Complete Behavior Guidebook*?

3. Priscilla Alderson (2008, 26) coined the phrase "human becomings" to describe our flawed approach to childhood. Think of ways that current practices of childcare invest in children as "human becomings." Now see if you can imagine ways to reinvent those practices that might focus on children in the present, as human beings.

4. The end of chapter 1 makes the claim that all human beings move from the culture of childhood into the culture of adulthood simply by passing days. Do you agree? Do you feel your work with young children holds implications for your membership in the culture of adulthood?

Chapter 2. "Poison Meat Eaters": The Social Lives of Children

1. What is a friend?

2. How do you know if someone is your friend?

3. Describe the qualities you look for in a friend.

4. Are children inherently social? Is it the adult's job to socialize children?

5. The book says, "Healthy friendships are built on an element of exclusion." Do you agree? Give an example that supports your belief.

6. Read the story at the end of chapter 2 by Lakisha Reid. Do you have a story (past or present) of children behaving in ways that seem strongly antisocial? If you were to look deeper, as Lakisha does in her story, can you think of another way to interpret the behavior of those children? Look for evidence of friendship and peer connection rather than disconnection. Ask your colleagues and peers for help in processing your story.

Chapter 3. "We're Stuck!": The Language of Childhood

1. Tell about a time when the play of children in your care reflected the realities they were experiencing in daily life.

2. How did you like to play as a child? What were your favorite games? Your favorite places? Your favorite activities? Do you do those things in any way anymore?

3. Do you consider yourself a playful adult? Do you find it easy to engage with children in their play scripts?

4. Think of your child care space. Are there "imitations" that you might consider swapping for the real thing?

Chapter 4. "It's Going to *Eat* Me!": Systems of Belief

1. Do you have any fears that others might categorize as "unrealistic?" What do you do when you encounter that fear? How do you work through it?

2. The Mary Howarth quote on page 95 talks about how we don't limit a child's color palette for painting, but in the ways in which we approach childhood, we often refuse to embrace the complexities of a child's emotional experience. How does this happen? In what ways does the culture of adulthood fail to recognize the light and dark that exists in a child's work? What examples can you provide?

3. Does your child care program have a "zero-tolerance policy"? How do you handle war and weapon play among children? Why?

4. I discuss four myths that motivate zero-tolerance policies. Which one most resonates with you? How does the information in this book challenge your thinking?

Chapter 5. "This Feels Amazing": Artistic Expression

1. Imagine the artifacts present right now in your early childhood setting. List them. Now imagine what artifacts the children might mention if they were listing the important creations in their environment. Are the lists different?

2. Think about your program. Are there aspects that function better with a product-oriented approach? What about aspects that function better with a process-oriented approach?

3. Kelly Matthews shares a story that highlights a time when a child's creative products resulted from a need in a play

script and served a function within the context of that play. Do you have a similar story about children in your program?

4. How often do children clean up in your program? Why?

Chapter 6. "Look at Me!": The Economics of Belonging

1. Recall a time when you were deeply sad and someone gave you the gift of his or her presence. What do you remember about that time?

2. Refer to Allison Pugh's quote: "Having 'nothing to say' is akin to not belonging, to a sort of unwelcome invisibility." In what ways do children in your program "have nothing to say"? Do you see evidence of children using their knowledge, abilities, material possessions, or experiences to secure belonging with peers?

3. What do you do when you are separated from loved ones? Are there ways you stay connected despite physical distance? Are there ways for the children in your care to stay connected with their loved ones while they are apart?

4. How do you respond to the idea that a child who is exhibiting "attention-seeking behavior" actually deserves attention? Do you agree?

Conclusion. "No One Remains Unchanged": Transformation

1. Reflect on David Sam and John Berry's statement that "no cultural group remains unchanged following culture contact." How are you changed because of your work with young children?

Resources by Chapter

EACH OF THE CHAPTERS IN THIS BOOK offers an introductory look at the various aspects of culture. For readers interested in digging deeper into any of these categories, the following resources offer fantastic next steps.

Chapter 1: Resources Offering a Background on Culture

- Michelle LaBaron and Venashri Pillay, eds., *Conflict across Cultures: A Unique Experience of Bridging Differences* (Boston: Intercultural Press, 2006). This edited volume of essays delivers an excellent look at the nature of culture and the ways in which culture affects daily life.

- John Monaghan and Peter Just, *Social and Cultural Anthropology: A Very Short Introduction* (Oxford: Oxford University Press, 2000), and Steve Bruce, *Sociology: A Very Short Introduction* (Oxford: Oxford University Press, 2000). In my research for this book, I discovered a series of volumes described as very short introductions, which offer exactly what they claim: very short introductions to different topics. The two that I would recommend to readers of this book are the introduction to social and cultural anthropology and the introduction to sociology. The field of early childhood education will grow richer as it broadens to include voices from other disciplines, particularly these two.

Chapter 2: Resources on Peer Groups and Friendship

- William Corsaro, *"We're Friends, Right?": Inside Kids' Culture* (Washington, DC: Joseph Henry Press, 2003). Corsaro's excellent book on children's friendships and peer culture is easy to read and full of stories and examples that illustrate effectively the nature of social connections among children.

- Ruth Forbes, *Beginning to Play: Young Children from Birth to Three* (Maidenhead, UK: Open University Press, 2004). Ruth Forbes's book centers on the play of very young children, and includes sections on the social interactions of infants, particularly the connections that these very young children have with their care providers.

Chapter 3: Resources about Play

- Stuart Brown, *Play: How It Shapes the Brain, Opens the Imagination, and Invigorates the Soul* (New York: Avery, 2010). This book is as much about the importance of play in the life of adults as it is about play for young children. For early childhood educators especially, the need to reconnect with our ability to play is urgent, and this book is an exceptional tool.

- Gaye Gronlund, *Developmentally Appropriate Play: Guiding Young Children to a Higher Level* (St. Paul, MN: Redleaf Press, 2010). I read Gronlund's book in nearly one sitting several years ago as a family child care provider. Her book had a profound impact on my practice as it was full of tools and strategies.

- Elizabeth Jones and Gretchen Reynolds, *The Play's the Thing: Teachers' Roles in Children's Play* (New York: Teachers College Press, 2011). When I became a family child care provider, one of my biggest questions was what to do while the children played. I knew that lots of unstructured time for play was important for children, but I couldn't help feeling like a bystander or an accessory. Jones and Reynolds's book illustrates many different dispositions that teachers might adopt with young children who are playing, identifying key roles that can help children get the most out of their play experiences. This book continues to be an indispensable resource for my work in the field of early childhood education.

- Elizabeth Jones and Renatta M. Cooper, *Playing to Get Smart* (New York: Teachers College Press, 2006). This book is a wonderful complement to *The Play's the Thing*. It addresses complex issues of play, including power, complexity, diversity, and good guy/bad guy themes. Beyond the argument that play is useful for helping children develop academic intelligence, this book looks at the competencies that children nurture through play in a broad array of areas.

Chapter 4: Resources about Children's Belief Systems

- Steven Popper, *Rethinking Superhero and Weapon Play* (Maidenhead, UK: Open University Press, 2013). Popper's book offers an exceptional look at superhero and weapon play, inquiring into the themes that children learn for life from their experiences with these scripts. Particularly intriguing to me were the sections about the assumptions that girls learn weak or passive roles through superhero scripts, as well as his sections about moral development of young children. His book was an eye-opener and I highly recommend reading it.

- Penny Holland, *We Don't Play with Guns Here: War, Weapon and Superhero Play in the Early Years* (Maidenhead, UK: Open University Press, 2003). A quick read, this book digs deeply into the myths surrounding war and weapon play, and thoughtfully explores relevant scientific research. What I appreciated was Holland's frank and honest discussion of her own personal discomfort and caution concerning children's pretend violent play as I shared her perspective and felt like I could relate to what she struggled to understand.

Chapter 5: Resources about Process-Oriented Approaches to Early Childhood

- Elizabeth Jones and Gretchen Reynolds, *The Play's the Thing: Teachers' Roles in Children's Play* (New York: Teachers College Press, 2011). This book is not only a helpful resource for learning more about play, but it also includes an insightful section on thinking about the way we manage time. In a few pages at the end of chapter 2, the authors tell of an experiment in which a school "untimed the curriculum"—removing watches, clocks, or any time-telling device to see what would happen, following the children's cues for when they were hungry, tired, or ready to move on to a different game. To find out what happened, you'll have to read the book.

For ideas of how to encourage a process-oriented approach to early childhood environments:

- Ann Pelo, *The Language of Art: Inquiry-Based Studio Practices in Early Childhood Settings* (St. Paul, MN: Redleaf Press, 2007).

- Margie Carter and Deb Curtis, *Learning Together with Young Children: A Curriculum Framework for Reflective Teachers* (St. Paul, MN: Redleaf Press, 2007).

Chapter 6: Resources about Belonging and Relationship

- Alfie Kohn, *Unconditional Parenting: Moving from Rewards and Punishments to Love and Reason* (New York: Atria Books, 2005). Written for parents, this book makes a clear and compelling case for styles of working with young children that are free from manipulation. No time-outs, no bribes, no sticker charts.

- Allison Pugh, *Longing and Belonging: Parents, Children, and Consumer Culture* (Berkeley: University of California Press, 2009). Pugh's book is more academic and based on her research with children in elementary school, but her findings resonate with those in early childhood as well. She articulates the role of childhood possessions as a means to secure belonging and relationships, and articulates the deep desire all children have to be connected to a community.

References

Ahn, Junehui. 2011. "'You're My Friend Today, but Not Tomorrow': Learning to Be Friends among Young U.S. Middle-Class Children." *American Ethnologist: Journal of the American Ethnological Society* 38 (2): 294–306.

Alderson, Priscilla. 2008. *Young Children's Rights: Exploring Beliefs, Principles and Practice*. Second Edition. Jessica Kingsley Publishers.

Arai, Tatsushi. 2006. "A Journey toward Cultural Fluency." In LeBaron and Pillay, *Conflict Across Cultures*, 57–82.

Brown, Stuart, with Christopher Vaughan. 2010. *Play: How It Shapes the Brain, Opens the Imagination, and Invigorates the Soul*. New York: Avery.

Carlson, Frances M. 2011. *Big Body Play: Why Boisterous, Vigorous, and Very Physical Play Is Essential to Children's Development and Learning*. Washington, D.C: National Association for the Education of Young Children.

Carter, Margie. 2008. "Encouraging a New View of Toddlers." *Exchange*, July/August, 38–40.

Corsaro, William A. 2011. *The Sociology of Childhood*. 3rd ed. Thousand Oaks, CA: SAGE Publications.

Forbes, Ruth. 2004. *Beginning to Play: Young Children From Birth to Three*. Maidenhead, UK: Open University Press.

Fowles, Jib. 1999. *The Case for Television Violence*. Thousand Oaks, CA: SAGE Publications.

Ginott, Dr Haim G. 2003. *Between Parent and Child: The Bestselling Classic That Revolutionized Parent-Child Communication*. Ed. Alice Ginott and H. Wallace Goddard. Rev updated ed. New York: Harmony.

Goode, David. 1994. *A World without Words: The Social Construction of Children Born Deaf and Blind*. Philadelphia: Temple University Press.

Gopnik, Alison. 2009. *The Philosophical Baby: What Children's Minds Tell Us About Truth, Love, and the Meaning of Life*. New York: Picador.

Gopnik, Alison, Andrew N. Meltzoff, and Patricia K. Kuhl. 2001. *The Scientist in the Crib: What Early Learning Tells Us About the Mind*. New York: William Morrow Paperbacks.

Hirsh-Pasek, Kathy, and Roberta Golinkoff. 2003. *Einstein Never Used Flashcards: How Our Children Really Learn—and Why They Need to Play More and Memorize Less*. Emmaus, PA: Rodale Books.

Holland, Penny. 2003. *We Don't Play with Guns Here: War, Weapon and Superhero Play in the Early Years*. Maidenhead, UK: Open University Press.

Howarth, Mary. 1989. "Rediscovering the Power of Fairy Tales: They Help Children Understand Their Lives." *Young Children* 45 (1): 58–65.

Hughes, Fergus P. 2009. *Children, Play, and Development*. 4th ed. Los Angeles: SAGE Publications.

Hutchby, Ian, and Jo Moran-Ellis, eds. 2005. *Children and Social Competence: Arenas of Action*. London: Routledge.

James, Allison. 1993. *Childhood Identities: Self and Social Relationships in the Experience of the Child*. Edinburgh: Edinburgh University Press.

James, Allison, and Alan Prout, eds. 2015. *Constructing and Reconstructing Childhood: Contemporary Issues in the Sociological Study of Childhood*. 3rd ed. London: Routledge.

Jones, Elizabeth, and Renatta M. Cooper. 2006. *Playing to Get Smart*. New York: Teachers College Press.

Jones, Elizabeth, and Gretchen Reynolds. 2011. *The Play's the Thing: Teachers' Roles in Children's Play*. New York: Teachers College Press.

Jones, Gerard. 2002. *Killing Monsters: Why Children Need Fantasy, Super Heroes, and Make-Believe Violence*. New York: Basic Books.

Karp, Harvey. 2008. *The Happiest Toddler on the Block: How to Eliminate Tantrums and Raise a Patient, Respectful, and Cooperative One- to Four-Year-Old*. New York, N.Y: Bantam.

Kohn, Alfie. 2005. *Unconditional Parenting: Moving from Rewards and Punishments to Love and Reason*. New York: Atria Books.

Leeman, Michael, Bev Bos, and Tom Hunter. 2004. *We've Been Waiting for You*. Turn the Page Press. Compact disc.

Løkken, Gunvor. 2000. "Tracing the Social Style of Toddler Peers." *Scandinavian Journal of Educational Research* 44 (2): 163–76.

Maslow, Abraham H. 1966. *The Psychology of Science, A Reconnaissance*. Chicago: Henry Regnery Co.

Matthews, Kelly, interview with Emily Plank. 2015. "Helping Children Say Goodbye Without Distracting." Accessed November 18, 2015. http://abundantlifechildren.com/2015/09/03/helping-children-say-goodbye-without-distracting/.

Mercogliano, Chris. 2008. *In Defense of Childhood: Protecting Kids' Inner Wildness.* Boston: Beacon Press.

Mintz, Steven. 2004. *Huck's Raft: A History of American Childhood.* Cambridge, MA: Belknap Press.

Monaghan, John, and Peter Just. 2000. *Social and Cultural Anthropology: A Very Short Introduction.* Oxford: Oxford University Press.

Paley, Vivian Gussin. 1986. "On Listening to What the Children Say." *Harvard Educational Review* 56 (2): 122–31.

Pillay, Venashri. 2006. "Culture: Exploring the River." In LeBaron and Pillay, *Conflict Across Cultures,* 22–25.

Plucker, Jonathan A. 2007. "John B. Watson (1878–1958) - Popularizing Behaviorism, The Little Albert Study, The 'Dozen Healthy Infants,' Life after the University." Accessed May 12, 2015. http://education. stateuniversity.com/pages/2543/Watson-John-B-1878-1958.html.

Popper, Steven. 2013. *Rethinking Superhero and Weapon Play.* Maidenhead: UK: Open University Press.

Pugh, Allison. 2009. *Longing and Belonging: Parents, Children, and Consumer Culture.* Berkeley: University of California Press.

Rogoff, Barbara. 2003. *The Cultural Nature of Human Development.* Oxford: Oxford University Press.

Sam, David L., and John W. Berry. 2010. "Acculturation When Individuals and Groups of Different Cultural Backgrounds Meet." *Perspectives on Psychological Science* 5 (4): 472–81.

Schildkrout, Enid. 2002. "Age and Gender in Hausa Society: Socio-Economic Roles of Children in Urban Kano." *Childhood* 9 (3): 342–68.

Schneier, Bruce. 2011. "The Security Mirage." Presented at TEDxPSU, April. http://www.ted.com/talks/bruce_schneier/transcript.

Shumaker, Heather. 2012. *It's OK Not to Share and Other Renegade Rules for Raising Competent and Compassionate Kids.* New York: Tarcher.

Skenazy, Lenore. 2013. "Why Does an Old-Fashioned Childhood Sound So Dangerous?" Keynote address presented at the It's Child's Play . . . and It Matters! Conference, Lindsay, Ontario, Canada, October 18.

Solomon, Andrew. 2013. *Far From the Tree: Parents, Children and the Search for Identity.* New York: Scribner.

Sunderland, Margot. 2008. *The Science of Parenting.* New York: DK.

Index

191